Unlocking E-Commerce Growth

Mastering Online Business with Technology-Driven Strategies

Jane Austen

Unlocking E-Commerce Growth

*© Copyright 2024 by **Jane Austen***

Chapter 1: Introduction to E-Commerce

The Evolution of Online Business

The evolution of online business is a fascinating journey that reflects the dynamic interplay between technology, consumer behavior, and market adaptation. It has transformed from a niche interest to a dominant force in the global economy, reshaping how goods and services are bought and sold. Understanding this evolution provides valuable insights into the current landscape of e-commerce and hints at future trends.

The story of online business begins in the early 1990s, when the internet was still in its infancy. At that time, the World Wide Web was a novel concept, and only a handful of visionaries foresaw its potential as a commercial platform. One of the earliest examples of online commerce was the sale of a Sting CD by the online retailer NetMarket in 1994. This humble transaction marked the first secure online purchase, paving the way for a new era of digital commerce.

As the internet grew, so did the possibilities for online business. The late 1990s saw the emergence of pioneering companies like Amazon and eBay, which capitalized on the growing accessibility of the internet. Amazon started as an online bookstore, leveraging the advantages of unlimited virtual shelf space and a global audience. eBay introduced the concept of online auctions, creating a dynamic marketplace where individuals could buy and sell goods. These companies set the stage for the rapid growth of e-commerce by embracing the technological advancements of the time.

The dot-com boom of the late 1990s and early 2000s was a period of exuberant growth and experimentation in online business. Entrepreneurs and investors flocked to the digital frontier, eager to capitalize on the internet's potential. While many ventures were short-lived, this period laid the groundwork for the e-commerce giants we know today. It was a time of innovation, with companies experimenting with various business models, from online marketplaces to subscription services.

The burst of the dot-com bubble in 2000 served as a sobering moment for the tech industry. Many companies failed, but those that survived emerged stronger and more resilient. The surviving businesses learned valuable lessons about sustainable growth and the importance of a solid business model. This era of reflection and recalibration set the stage for the next phase of online business evolution.

The mid-2000s marked the rise of social media and mobile technology, both of which had profound impacts on online business. Social media platforms like Facebook, Twitter, and Instagram created new opportunities for businesses to engage with customers and build brand loyalty. These platforms became essential tools for marketing and customer interaction, allowing businesses to reach audiences in previously unimaginable ways.

Mobile technology further revolutionized online business by making e-commerce accessible anytime and anywhere. The proliferation of smartphones and tablets enabled consumers to shop on the go, leading to the rise of mobile commerce. Businesses had to adapt by optimizing their websites for mobile devices and developing user-friendly apps. This shift towards mobile-first strategies became a defining characteristic of the modern e-commerce landscape.

The late 2000s and early 2010s saw the emergence of new business models and technologies that further reshaped online commerce. Subscription services gained popularity, offering everything from streaming media to monthly curated boxes. Companies like Netflix and Birchbox demonstrated the power of recurring revenue models, providing consumers with convenience and personalized experiences.

Simultaneously, advancements in logistics and supply chain management improved the efficiency and reliability of online business. Companies like Amazon invested heavily in warehouse automation and delivery infrastructure, enabling faster shipping and enhanced customer service. These innovations raised consumer expectations for quick and seamless shopping experiences, prompting businesses to prioritize operational efficiency.

The evolution of online business has also been characterized by the integration of data-driven strategies. Businesses now have access to vast amounts of consumer data, which they use to personalize marketing efforts, optimize inventory management, and enhance customer experiences. Data analytics has become an indispensable tool for making informed decisions and staying competitive in the digital marketplace.

As we move into the present day, online business continues to evolve at a rapid pace. The global pandemic of 2020 accelerated the adoption of e-commerce as consumers turned to online shopping in unprecedented numbers. This shift has highlighted the importance of agility and adaptability in the face of changing circumstances. Businesses that can quickly pivot and embrace new technologies are better positioned to thrive in the ever-evolving digital landscape.

The future of online business promises even more innovation and transformation. Emerging technologies such as virtual reality, augmented reality, and blockchain hold the potential to redefine how consumers interact with online businesses. Virtual reality could create immersive shopping experiences, while blockchain offers enhanced security and transparency in transactions. As these technologies mature, they will likely open new avenues for growth and engagement in the e-commerce sector.

Reflecting on the evolution of online business offers valuable lessons for those entering the field. The journey from the early days of the internet to today's digital economy underscores the importance of adaptability, innovation, and customer-centricity. Successful online businesses have thrived by embracing change, leveraging technology, and understanding the needs and preferences of their customers.

For newcomers to the world of e-commerce, understanding this evolution is not just about appreciating the past; it's about preparing for the future. The landscape of online business is constantly shifting, and staying informed about trends and technological advancements is crucial for success. By learning from the experiences of those who came before, aspiring entrepreneurs can navigate the challenges and opportunities of the digital marketplace with confidence and foresight.

Key Drivers of E-Commerce Growth

The growth of e-commerce has been nothing short of meteoric, fueled by a confluence of technological advancements, shifting consumer behaviors, and strategic business innovations. Understanding the key drivers behind this growth is crucial for anyone looking to succeed in the digital marketplace. These drivers not only illuminate the past trajectory of e-commerce but also provide insights into the future potential of online business.

One of the most significant drivers of e-commerce growth is the widespread adoption of the internet and digital technology. As internet penetration has increased globally, more consumers have gained access to online shopping platforms. The convenience of accessing a vast array of products and services from the comfort of one's home has revolutionized the retail experience. This accessibility has broken down geographical barriers, allowing businesses to reach customers far beyond their local markets. The internet has effectively expanded the customer base for e-commerce businesses, enabling them to tap into global demand.

The proliferation of mobile devices has further accelerated the growth of e-commerce. Smartphones and tablets have become ubiquitous, providing consumers with the ability to shop anytime, anywhere. Mobile commerce, or m-commerce, has emerged as a powerful force in the online retail landscape. Businesses have responded by optimizing their websites for mobile use and developing user-friendly apps that enhance the shopping experience. The convenience of mobile shopping, combined with features like mobile payment options and location-based services, has made it easier than ever for consumers to make purchases on the go.

Consumer behavior has also played a pivotal role in driving e-commerce growth. Today's consumers are more connected, informed, and discerning than ever before. They seek convenience, variety, and value, and they use digital tools to compare products, read reviews, and make informed purchasing decisions. The rise of social media has amplified this trend, as consumers increasingly turn to platforms like Instagram and Facebook for product recommendations and inspiration. Businesses that understand and cater to these digitally-savvy consumers can capture a significant share of the e-commerce market.

Personalization is another key driver of e-commerce growth. Consumers expect tailored experiences that reflect their individual preferences and needs. Advances in data analytics and artificial intelligence have enabled businesses to gather insights into consumer behavior and deliver personalized recommendations, offers, and content. This level of personalization enhances customer satisfaction and loyalty, driving repeat business and increasing sales. By leveraging data to create personalized experiences, e-commerce businesses can differentiate themselves in a competitive market.

Logistics and supply chain innovations have also contributed to the rapid growth of e-commerce. Efficient logistics operations are critical to meeting consumer expectations for fast and reliable delivery. Companies like Amazon have set the standard with innovations such as same-day and next-day delivery, forcing other businesses to improve their logistics capabilities. Advances in inventory management, warehousing, and transportation have streamlined the supply chain, reducing costs and improving service levels. These improvements have made e-commerce a viable option for a broader range of products, from groceries to high-end electronics.

The digital payment landscape has evolved significantly, supporting the growth of e-commerce by providing secure and convenient payment options. Payment gateways, digital wallets, and contactless payment methods have made it easier for consumers to complete transactions online. These innovations have addressed concerns about security and fraud, building consumer confidence in online shopping. As digital payment solutions continue to evolve, they will further facilitate e-commerce growth by offering consumers more flexibility and convenience in their purchasing decisions.

Government policies and regulations have also influenced the growth of e-commerce. In many regions, supportive policies have created a favorable environment for online business. Tax incentives, infrastructure development, and investment in digital literacy programs have encouraged the growth of e-commerce ecosystems. However, regulatory challenges remain, such as issues related to data privacy, cybersecurity, and cross-border trade. Navigating these challenges requires businesses to stay informed about regulatory changes and adapt their strategies accordingly.

The COVID-19 pandemic has had a profound impact on e-commerce growth. As lockdowns and social distancing measures were implemented worldwide, consumers turned to online shopping out of necessity. This surge in demand accelerated the adoption of e-commerce across various sectors, from fashion to grocery. Businesses that were able to pivot quickly to online channels thrived, while those without a digital presence faced significant challenges. The pandemic has reshaped consumer behavior and expectations, with many of the changes likely to persist in the post-pandemic world.

Innovation in marketing and customer engagement has driven e-commerce growth by enabling businesses to reach and connect with consumers in new ways. Digital marketing strategies, such as search engine optimization (SEO), pay-per-click (PPC) advertising, and social media marketing, have become essential tools for attracting and retaining customers. Content marketing and brand storytelling have also gained prominence, allowing businesses to build strong emotional connections with their audiences. By crafting compelling narratives and engaging content, e-commerce businesses can differentiate themselves and foster brand loyalty.

The future of e-commerce growth will be shaped by the continued evolution of these key drivers. Technological advancements, such as virtual reality, augmented reality, and the Internet of Things (IoT), will create new opportunities for immersive and interactive shopping experiences. Sustainability and ethical considerations will also play an increasingly important role, as consumers become more conscious of the environmental and social impact of their purchases. Businesses that can adapt to these trends and leverage new technologies will be well-positioned to capitalize on the ongoing growth of e-commerce.

In conclusion, the growth of e-commerce is driven by a complex interplay of technological, consumer, logistical, and regulatory factors. By understanding these drivers, businesses can develop strategies that align with the evolving landscape of online commerce. As the e-commerce industry continues to transform, staying attuned to these key drivers will be essential for achieving success in the digital marketplace.

The Impact of Technology on Retail

Technology's impact on retail has been transformative, reshaping every aspect of how businesses operate and consumers shop. From the way products are marketed to the efficiency of supply chains, technology has driven innovation and efficiency, making it an indispensable component of the modern retail landscape.

One of the most profound changes technology has brought to retail is the digitization of the shopping experience. The rise of e-commerce platforms has allowed consumers to shop from anywhere in the world, at any time, with just a few clicks. This shift has expanded the reach of retailers beyond physical store locations, opening up global markets and increasing sales opportunities. The convenience of online shopping has become a significant factor in consumer decision-making, as customers can easily compare products, read reviews, and make informed purchases from the comfort of their homes.

In brick-and-mortar stores, technology has enhanced the in-store experience through innovations such as digital signage, interactive kiosks, and mobile point-of-sale systems. These advancements have streamlined the shopping process, reducing wait times and improving customer service. Retailers can now offer personalized recommendations and promotions in real-time, tailoring the shopping experience to individual preferences. This level of personalization is made possible by collecting and analyzing customer data, enabling retailers to understand and anticipate consumer needs.

The use of data analytics has become a cornerstone of modern retail strategy. Retailers now have access to vast amounts of data, from customer demographics to purchasing behavior. By analyzing this data, retailers can identify trends, optimize inventory levels, and make data-driven decisions that enhance profitability. Predictive analytics allows businesses to forecast demand more accurately, reducing the risk of overstocking or stockouts. This level of insight has transformed inventory management, making it more efficient and responsive to changing market conditions.

Supply chain operations have also been revolutionized by technology. Automation and robotics have streamlined warehousing and logistics, reducing costs and improving accuracy. Technologies such as RFID and IoT devices provide real-time visibility into inventory levels and product locations, facilitating better coordination across the supply chain. These innovations have enabled retailers to offer faster delivery times and more reliable service, meeting the heightened expectations of today's consumers.

Mobile technology has further reshaped the retail landscape by enabling the rise of mobile commerce, or m-commerce. With smartphones and tablets, consumers can shop on-the-go, making purchases whenever and wherever they choose. Retailers have responded by developing mobile-optimized websites and apps that offer seamless navigation and secure payment options. Mobile devices have also become powerful tools for enhancing the in-store experience, with features such as mobile coupons, loyalty programs, and in-app shopping lists.

Social media has emerged as a powerful marketing channel for retailers, enabling them to reach and engage with consumers in new and creative ways. Platforms like Instagram, Facebook, and Pinterest allow retailers to showcase their products through visually appealing content and storytelling. Social media influencers and brand ambassadors have become key players in shaping consumer perceptions and driving sales. By leveraging social media, retailers can build brand awareness, foster customer loyalty, and create a sense of community around their products.

Augmented reality (AR) and virtual reality (VR) technologies are beginning to make their mark on the retail industry as well. AR applications allow consumers to visualize products in their own environments, enhancing their confidence in online purchases. For example, furniture retailers use AR to enable customers to see how a piece of furniture would look in their home before buying. VR, on the other hand, offers immersive experiences that can transport consumers into virtual storefronts or fashion shows, creating unique and memorable interactions.

The rise of technology has also brought about new challenges for retailers, particularly in the areas of data security and privacy. As retailers collect and store more consumer data, they must ensure that this information is protected from breaches and unauthorized access. Compliance with data protection regulations, such as the General Data Protection Regulation (GDPR), is essential for maintaining consumer trust and avoiding legal repercussions. Retailers must invest in robust cybersecurity measures and transparent privacy policies to safeguard customer information.

Artificial intelligence and machine learning have begun to play a crucial role in enhancing retail operations. These technologies can automate routine tasks, such as customer service inquiries and inventory management, freeing up human resources for more strategic activities. AI-powered chatbots provide instant customer support, answering questions and guiding consumers through the purchasing process. Machine learning algorithms can analyze data to identify patterns and optimize pricing strategies, ensuring that retailers remain competitive in a dynamic market.

As technology continues to evolve, the future of retail will likely be characterized by even greater integration and innovation. The development of smart stores, where every aspect of the shopping experience is connected and automated, is already underway. These stores leverage IoT devices, AI, and data analytics to provide personalized experiences, optimize operations, and create a frictionless shopping environment. Consumers can expect more intuitive and engaging interactions with retailers as technology becomes increasingly embedded in every aspect of the retail journey.

In conclusion, the impact of technology on retail has been transformative, driving innovation and efficiency across the industry. From digitizing the shopping experience to optimizing supply chains, technology has enabled retailers to meet the evolving needs and expectations of consumers. As technology continues to advance, retailers must remain agile and forward-thinking, embracing new tools and strategies to maintain their competitive edge in a rapidly changing landscape. By harnessing the power of technology, retailers can create value for both their customers and their businesses, ensuring their success in the digital age.

Consumer Behavior in the Digital Age

Understanding consumer behavior in the digital age is an intricate tapestry woven from technological advancements, shifting cultural norms, and evolving individual preferences. In this era, the way consumers interact with brands, make purchasing decisions, and express loyalty has undergone a dramatic transformation, demanding a fresh perspective from businesses aiming to thrive in an increasingly competitive market.

At the heart of this transformation lies the unprecedented access to information. With the internet at their fingertips, consumers today are more informed than ever before. They diligently research products and services, compare prices, and read reviews before making a purchase decision. This empowerment has shifted the balance of power, allowing consumers to dictate terms and expect a higher level of transparency and accountability from brands. Businesses must recognize this change and ensure they provide clear, accurate, and comprehensive information to meet these heightened expectations.

Social media has emerged as a pivotal factor in shaping consumer behavior. These platforms are not only tools for communication but also powerful channels for influence and discovery. Consumers turn to social media to seek recommendations, share experiences, and engage with brands on a more personal level. The lines between consumers and marketers have blurred, as individuals become brand advocates, creating user-generated content that carries authenticity and trust. For businesses, maintaining an active and genuine presence on social media is crucial to building relationships and fostering brand loyalty.

Another significant aspect of consumer behavior in the digital age is the demand for personalization. Modern consumers expect tailored experiences that resonate with their unique preferences and needs. Personalization extends beyond mere product recommendations; it encompasses every interaction a consumer has with a brand. From personalized email campaigns to customized shopping experiences, businesses must leverage data insights to create meaningful connections that enhance customer satisfaction and loyalty. A one-size-fits-all approach is no longer sufficient in a world where consumers crave individuality.

Convenience has become a paramount consideration for consumers, influencing their purchasing decisions more than ever. The proliferation of e-commerce and mobile technology has set new standards for convenience, with consumers expecting seamless and frictionless experiences. Whether it's the ability to make a purchase with a single click or the convenience of same-day delivery, businesses that prioritize convenience can capture the attention and loyalty of time-strapped consumers. Streamlining processes and eliminating barriers to purchase are essential strategies for success in the digital marketplace.

The role of trust and authenticity in consumer behavior cannot be overstated. In an era where information is abundant, consumers are increasingly discerning about the brands they choose to support. Authenticity has become a key differentiator, with consumers gravitating towards brands that align with their values and demonstrate genuine commitment to social and environmental responsibility. Businesses must cultivate trust by being transparent about their practices, engaging in ethical marketing, and actively participating in initiatives that resonate with their audience.

The concept of the customer journey has evolved significantly in the digital age. No longer a linear path, the customer journey is now a complex web of interactions across multiple touchpoints. From initial awareness to post-purchase engagement, consumers move fluidly between online and offline channels, seeking a seamless and cohesive experience. Businesses must map out these touchpoints and ensure they deliver consistent messaging and value at every stage of the journey. Omnichannel strategies that integrate digital and physical experiences are essential to meeting the diverse needs of contemporary consumers.

In addition to these shifts, the digital age has also given rise to new consumer segments, each with distinct behaviors and preferences. Millennials and Generation Z, for instance, have grown up immersed in technology and are adept at navigating the digital landscape. They prioritize experiences over products, value social and environmental consciousness, and seek brands that offer authenticity and innovation. Understanding the nuances of these consumer segments allows businesses to tailor their strategies and offerings to resonate with their target audience.

As consumer behavior continues to evolve, businesses must adopt a mindset of continuous learning and adaptation. Staying attuned to emerging trends, technological advancements, and cultural shifts is vital to remaining relevant and competitive. This requires a proactive approach to gathering and analyzing data, embracing innovation, and fostering a culture of experimentation. By being agile and responsive, businesses can anticipate changes in consumer behavior and position themselves as leaders in the digital marketplace.

Incorporating feedback into the business strategy is another critical aspect of understanding consumer behavior. Consumers today are vocal about their experiences, and their feedback provides valuable insights into what is working and what needs improvement. Businesses that actively listen and respond to consumer feedback can refine their products, services, and customer experiences, leading to increased satisfaction and loyalty. Creating channels for open communication and demonstrating a willingness to act on feedback are essential components of a customer-centric approach.

The digital age presents both challenges and opportunities for businesses seeking to understand and influence consumer behavior. By recognizing the complexities and nuances of modern consumer behavior, businesses can develop strategies that resonate with their audience and drive long-term success. Embracing technology, prioritizing personalization, and cultivating trust are all integral to thriving in this dynamic landscape. As consumer expectations continue to evolve, businesses that remain adaptable and customer-focused will be well-positioned to navigate the ever-changing digital terrain.

Overview of E-Commerce Models

E-commerce has revolutionized the way businesses operate and consumers shop, offering a plethora of models that cater to different market needs and preferences. Understanding these models is crucial for any aspiring entrepreneur looking to carve out a niche in the digital marketplace. Each model has its unique characteristics, advantages, and challenges, and selecting the right one requires a careful evaluation of business goals, target audience, and resources.

One of the most prominent e-commerce models is the Business-to-Consumer (B2C) model. It involves transactions between businesses and individual consumers. This model is familiar to most people, as it mirrors traditional retail shopping but in an online setting. Companies like Amazon and Zappos exemplify the B2C model, offering a wide range of products directly to consumers through their digital storefronts. The B2C model thrives on high-volume sales and efficient logistics. Businesses employing this model must focus on creating an engaging user experience, streamlining the purchasing process, and providing excellent customer service to retain consumer loyalty.

The Business-to-Business (B2B) model, on the other hand, involves transactions between businesses. In this model, companies sell products or services to other businesses rather than individual consumers. B2B e-commerce often involves bulk orders, long-term contracts, and negotiated pricing. Alibaba is a well-known example of a B2B platform, connecting manufacturers and wholesalers with buyers across the globe. The B2B model requires a deep understanding of client needs and purchasing processes, as well as the ability to build strong relationships with business clients. Successful B2B companies prioritize efficiency, reliability, and personalized service to meet the demands of their corporate customers.

Consumer-to-Consumer (C2C) e-commerce enables individuals to sell products or services to each other, usually through a third-party platform that facilitates the transaction. Online marketplaces like eBay and Etsy are classic examples of C2C platforms, where users can list items for sale and connect with potential buyers. The appeal of the C2C model lies in its ability to empower individuals to participate in commerce without the need for a formal business structure. However, it also presents challenges such as ensuring transaction security and maintaining trust between buyers and sellers. Platforms operating in the C2C space must implement robust systems for managing disputes and verifying user credibility to foster a safe and reliable marketplace environment.

Another notable model is the Consumer-to-Business (C2B) model, where individuals offer products or services to businesses. This model is less common but has gained traction with the rise of the gig economy and freelance platforms. Websites like Upwork and Freelancer facilitate C2B transactions by connecting freelancers with companies seeking specific skills or services. The C2B model allows individuals to monetize their expertise and offers businesses access to a flexible workforce. Companies utilizing this model must focus on identifying the right talent, managing project timelines, and ensuring quality deliverables to maximize the benefits of C2B interactions.

Subscription-based e-commerce has emerged as a popular model, offering consumers regular access to products or services in exchange for a recurring fee. This model spans various industries, from media streaming services like Netflix to monthly subscription boxes like Birchbox. The subscription model provides businesses with a steady revenue stream and fosters customer loyalty through ongoing engagement. However, it requires a commitment to continually deliver value and adapt to changing consumer preferences. Successful subscription businesses focus on personalization, exclusive content, and seamless user experiences to retain subscribers and reduce churn.

Direct-to-Consumer (DTC) e-commerce is another model that has gained prominence in recent years. It involves brands selling their products directly to consumers, bypassing traditional retail channels. This model allows businesses to control their brand narrative, gather valuable customer data, and build direct relationships with their audience. Companies like Warby Parker and Glossier have successfully leveraged the DTC model to disrupt established industries and create unique brand identities. The DTC model demands a strong online presence, effective digital marketing strategies, and a deep understanding of consumer behavior to succeed in a competitive landscape.

Dropshipping is a unique e-commerce model where the retailer does not hold inventory. Instead, when a customer places an order, the retailer purchases the item from a third-party supplier, who then ships it directly to the customer. This model reduces the financial risk and operational burden associated with inventory management, making it an attractive option for entrepreneurs with limited resources. However, dropshipping also presents challenges in terms of quality control, shipping times, and supplier reliability. Retailers must carefully vet their suppliers and maintain open communication to ensure a positive customer experience.

Social commerce is an emerging model that leverages social media platforms to facilitate online shopping. By integrating e-commerce functionalities into social networks, businesses can engage with consumers in a more interactive and personalized manner. Instagram Shopping and Facebook Marketplace are examples of social commerce initiatives that enable users to discover and purchase products directly within the app. This model capitalizes on the power of social influence and peer recommendations, making it a valuable addition to a brand's e-commerce strategy. Businesses must cultivate an authentic social presence and create compelling content to thrive in the social commerce arena.

Affiliate marketing is another model that plays a significant role in the e-commerce ecosystem. It involves promoting products or services through affiliate partners who earn a commission for each sale generated through their referral links. This model allows businesses to expand their reach and tap into new audiences without the need for significant upfront investment. Affiliate marketing relies on building partnerships with influencers, bloggers, and content creators who align with the brand's values and target audience. Companies must establish clear guidelines and provide affiliates with the necessary tools and resources to drive successful campaigns.

Understanding these diverse e-commerce models is essential for entrepreneurs seeking to navigate the digital marketplace. Each model offers unique opportunities and challenges, and selecting the right one depends on a variety of factors, including target audience, business goals, and resources. By exploring these models and identifying the best fit for their business, entrepreneurs can position themselves for success in the ever-evolving world of e-commerce. With a clear understanding of the landscape and a strategic approach, businesses can harness the power of digital commerce to achieve their objectives and thrive in a competitive environment.

Chapter 2: Developing a Successful E-Commerce Strategy

Defining Your Business Goals

Defining business goals is a foundational step in the journey of entrepreneurship. It serves as a compass, guiding decisions and strategies, while providing a clear vision of what success looks like. Setting precise goals is essential for maintaining focus, measuring progress, and ensuring that every action taken aligns with the overarching mission of the business. As you embark on this process, consider the following aspects to effectively define and achieve your business objectives.

Begin by reflecting on your core motivations and values. Understanding why you are starting a business and what you hope to achieve is fundamental. Are you driven by a passion for a particular industry, a desire to solve a specific problem, or the aspiration to achieve financial independence? Your motivations will help shape your business goals and ensure they resonate with your personal and professional values. This alignment is crucial, as it will sustain your commitment and enthusiasm, even when faced with challenges.

Once you have a clear understanding of your motivations, it's time to articulate your long-term vision. What does success look like for your business in five, ten, or even twenty years? A compelling vision provides direction and inspiration, serving as a north star that guides your journey. It should be ambitious yet attainable, reflecting the impact you wish to make and the legacy you hope to leave. A well-defined vision sets the stage for establishing specific, measurable, achievable, relevant, and time-bound (SMART) goals that will help you realize your aspirations.

With your vision in mind, break it down into smaller, actionable goals. These goals should address various aspects of your business, including financial performance, market presence, customer satisfaction, and operational efficiency. For instance, a financial goal might involve achieving a certain revenue milestone, while a market goal could focus on expanding into new geographic regions. By segmenting your vision into manageable objectives, you create a roadmap that outlines the steps needed to achieve your long-term aspirations.

As you define your goals, ensure they are SMART. Specific goals provide clarity and precision, eliminating ambiguity and setting clear expectations. Measurable goals allow you to track progress and assess success, using quantifiable metrics to evaluate outcomes. Achievable goals consider your resources and constraints, ensuring that objectives are realistic and within reach. Relevant goals align with your overarching vision and mission, reinforcing your strategic priorities. Time-bound goals establish a clear timeline for achievement, creating a sense of urgency and focus.

Consider the resources at your disposal and identify potential challenges that may impact your ability to achieve your goals. Resources encompass financial capital, human resources, technology, and expertise. Understanding these elements will help you set realistic objectives and identify areas where additional investment or support may be needed. Similarly, anticipating potential challenges allows you to develop contingency plans and mitigate risks, enhancing your resilience and adaptability.

Engage stakeholders in the goal-setting process. Whether you have co-founders, employees, investors, or advisors, their input can provide valuable perspectives and insights. Collaborating with stakeholders fosters a sense of ownership and alignment, ensuring that everyone is committed to achieving the shared vision. Additionally, involving others in the process can uncover blind spots and generate innovative ideas, enriching your strategic planning.

Communicate your goals clearly and consistently to all members of your organization. Transparency fosters accountability and creates a shared understanding of what success looks like. Regularly update your team on progress and achievements, celebrating milestones and recognizing contributions. This not only boosts morale but also reinforces the importance of working towards common objectives.

Monitor progress regularly and be prepared to adjust your goals as necessary. The business landscape is dynamic, and unforeseen circumstances may require you to pivot or recalibrate your objectives. Flexibility is essential, as it allows you to respond to changes while remaining aligned with your long-term vision. Regularly reviewing and revising your goals ensures they remain relevant and achievable, guiding your business through periods of growth and transition.

Leverage data and analytics to inform your goal-setting process and track progress. Data-driven insights provide a comprehensive understanding of your business's performance, enabling you to make informed decisions and refine your strategies. By analyzing key metrics and trends, you can identify areas of strength and opportunities for improvement, optimizing your approach to achieve your goals.

Celebrate successes and learn from setbacks. Achieving your business goals is a journey with its highs and lows. Recognize and reward accomplishments, as they serve as motivation and validation of your efforts. Equally, view setbacks as learning opportunities, analyzing what went wrong and how you can improve. This mindset fosters a culture of continuous improvement and resilience, empowering you to overcome challenges and achieve your business objectives.

In defining your business goals, remember that they are not static. As your business evolves, so too will your objectives. Regularly revisit your goals to ensure they reflect your current circumstances and aspirations. This iterative process of reflection, planning, and adaptation will keep your business aligned with its vision, driving sustained growth and success. By setting clear, strategic goals, you lay the foundation for a thriving enterprise, equipped to navigate the complexities of the business world and achieve lasting impact.

Identifying Target Markets and Niches

Identifying target markets and niches is a critical step for any business aiming to carve out a successful path in today's competitive environment. The process involves understanding who your ideal customers are, what they need, and how your product or service can fulfill those needs more effectively than competitors can. This knowledge not only informs your marketing strategies but also your product development, pricing, and overall business operations, ensuring that every effort is aligned with your core audience.

To begin, consider starting with thorough market research. This involves gathering data on consumer demographics, preferences, behaviors, and purchasing patterns. Various tools and methods can be used for this purpose, such as surveys, focus groups, interviews, and analysis of existing market reports. These insights will help you gain a clearer picture of the market landscape and the segments that are most likely to resonate with your offerings.

Next, look at your current customer base, if applicable. Analyze who is already buying your product or service and what characteristics they share. This can provide valuable clues about your target market. Pay attention to factors such as age, gender, location, income level, education, lifestyle, and values. Understanding these elements will help you refine your target market and tailor your marketing messages to speak directly to their interests and needs.

Once you have a broad understanding of the market, it's time to segment it. Market segmentation involves dividing a broad market into smaller, more defined categories based on shared characteristics. Common segmentation criteria include demographic, psychographic, geographic, and behavioral factors. By segmenting the market, you can identify specific groups of consumers who are most likely to benefit from your product or service, allowing you to focus your efforts on the most promising opportunities.

When defining your target market, ensure it's large enough to sustain your business but not so broad that your marketing becomes diluted. A well-defined target market allows you to concentrate your resources on a specific group, increasing the effectiveness of your marketing campaigns and building stronger customer relationships. This focused approach often leads to higher conversion rates and customer loyalty, as your efforts are directed towards individuals who are most likely to engage with your brand.

Identifying a niche is an extension of the target market selection process, involving a deeper dive into specific needs and preferences within a broader market. A niche market is characterized by a distinct set of needs that are not being adequately addressed by mainstream providers. By focusing on a niche, you can position your business as a specialist, offering unique value and expertise that larger competitors may overlook. This specialization can create a competitive advantage, as niche markets often have less competition and more loyal customers.

To identify a viable niche, consider your own strengths, passions, and expertise. What unique skills or knowledge do you bring to the table? How can you leverage these attributes to address specific pain points or desires within your target market? By aligning your strengths with market needs, you can develop a compelling value proposition that differentiates your business from others.

Evaluate the competition within your chosen niche. Analyze what competitors are offering, their strengths and weaknesses, and how they position themselves in the market. This analysis will help you identify gaps or opportunities for differentiation, enabling you to refine your niche strategy and capitalize on unmet needs. Consider how you can offer superior value, whether through product features, customer service, pricing, or brand experience.

Once your target market and niche have been defined, develop buyer personas to further guide your marketing strategies. A buyer persona is a semi-fictional representation of your ideal customer, based on real data and insights. It includes details such as demographics, interests, challenges, and buying motivations. Creating detailed personas helps you humanize your target audience, allowing you to craft personalized and relevant marketing messages that resonate on a deeper level.

Tailor your marketing efforts to speak directly to your defined target market and niche. This involves using language, imagery, and channels that align with their preferences and behaviors. For example, younger audiences may respond better to digital marketing and social media, while older audiences might prefer traditional advertising methods. Understanding where and how your audience consumes information will enable you to reach them more effectively.

As your business grows and evolves, continuously reassess your target market and niche. Consumer preferences and market dynamics are always changing, and staying attuned to these shifts is essential for long-term success. Regularly review market data, customer feedback, and competitive trends to ensure your strategies remain relevant and impactful. This ongoing process of evaluation and adaptation will help you maintain a strong market position and seize new opportunities as they arise.

In summary, identifying target markets and niches requires a strategic approach that combines market research, segmentation, and a deep understanding of consumer needs. By focusing on specific segments and unmet needs, you can differentiate your business, build strong customer relationships, and achieve sustainable growth. Embrace the process of discovery and refinement, and you'll be well-equipped to navigate the complexities of the marketplace and create lasting value for your customers.

Crafting a Unique Value Proposition

A unique value proposition (UVP) is the cornerstone of any successful business strategy. It articulates the distinct benefits and advantages that your product or service offers, setting you apart in a crowded marketplace. Crafting a compelling UVP requires a deep understanding of your audience, your product, and the competitive landscape. This chapter will guide you through the essential steps to develop a UVP that resonates with your target market and positions your brand for success.

Begin by immersing yourself in the minds of your customers. To create a UVP that truly speaks to them, it's crucial to understand their needs, desires, and pain points. Conduct thorough market research, leveraging surveys, interviews, and focus groups to gather insights. Pay close attention to the language your customers use to describe their challenges and what solutions they are seeking. This information is invaluable in shaping a UVP that addresses their specific concerns and aspirations.

Once you have a clear understanding of your customers, turn your attention to your product or service. What makes it unique or superior? Consider the features, benefits, and emotional appeal that distinguish your offering from the competition. A strong UVP highlights not just the functional aspects of your product but also the emotional and experiential benefits it provides. Whether it's saving time, reducing stress, or enhancing lifestyle, these intangible elements can be powerful motivators for potential customers.

Next, conduct a competitive analysis to identify gaps and opportunities in the market. Study your competitors' offerings and their value propositions, noting where they excel and where they fall short. This analysis will help you pinpoint areas where you can differentiate your product and carve out a unique position. Look for unmet needs or underserved segments that your business can address more effectively than others.

With this foundation, begin drafting your UVP. It should be clear, concise, and compelling, capturing the essence of what makes your product valuable and different. A well-crafted UVP communicates the primary benefit of your product in a way that is easy to understand and remember. Avoid jargon or overly complex language; simplicity is key to ensuring your message resonates with your audience.

Consider using storytelling techniques to bring your UVP to life. Stories are powerful tools for conveying value and building emotional connections. Share anecdotes or testimonials that illustrate how your product has positively impacted customers' lives. Real-life examples make your UVP more relatable and tangible, helping potential customers envision the benefits they could experience.

As you refine your UVP, ensure it is aligned with your brand identity and positioning. Your UVP should reinforce the core values and mission of your business, creating a cohesive narrative that resonates across all touchpoints. Consistency is vital; your UVP should be reflected in your marketing materials, website, social media presence, and customer interactions. This alignment strengthens brand recognition and trust, fostering a deeper connection with your audience.

Test your UVP with real customers to gauge its effectiveness. Gather feedback on how it resonates and whether it communicates the intended benefits. Use this feedback to make adjustments and enhancements, ensuring your UVP is both compelling and accurate. This iterative process of testing and refining is crucial to developing a UVP that truly speaks to your target market.

Once your UVP is finalized, integrate it into your marketing and sales strategies. Use it as a guiding principle for crafting marketing messages, designing campaigns, and developing content. A strong UVP serves as a foundation for all your communication efforts, providing clarity and focus that helps differentiate your brand and attract the right customers.

Remember that a UVP is not static; it should evolve as your business grows and market dynamics change. Regularly revisit and reassess your UVP to ensure it remains relevant and competitive. Monitor industry trends, customer feedback, and competitor activities to identify opportunities for refinement and innovation. Staying attuned to these changes allows you to adapt your UVP and maintain a strong market position.

In conclusion, a unique value proposition is a vital component of your business strategy, offering a clear and compelling reason for customers to choose your product over others. By understanding your audience, leveraging your product's unique attributes, and differentiating from competitors, you can craft a UVP that resonates and drives success. Embrace this process with creativity and insight, and you'll lay the groundwork for a brand that stands out and thrives in the marketplace.

Competitive Analysis and Positioning

In the dynamic and often unpredictable world of business, understanding your competition and carving out a distinct market position is crucial for success. Competitive analysis and strategic positioning are the twin pillars that support your ability to stand out and thrive. These processes involve a deep dive into the competitive landscape, identifying strengths and weaknesses, and leveraging insights to inform your business strategy.

The journey begins with a comprehensive competitive analysis. This involves systematically identifying and evaluating your current and potential competitors. Start by listing direct competitors—those who offer similar products or services and target the same customer segments. But don't stop there; also consider indirect competitors who may not be in the same industry but fulfill similar customer needs. For example, a fitness app may have direct competitors in other fitness apps but indirect competitors in leisure activities like hiking or cycling.

Gather information about their offerings, pricing, market share, customer reviews, and marketing strategies. This can be done through various means such as browsing their websites, subscribing to their newsletters, and following them on social media. Industry reports, trade publications, and customer feedback are also valuable sources of information. The goal is to build a comprehensive understanding of who your competitors are and what they bring to the table.

As you analyze this data, pay special attention to the unique selling propositions (USPs) of your competitors. What makes them stand out in the eyes of their customers? Identifying their USPs can reveal gaps in the market or areas where your competitors excel. This insight is invaluable for identifying opportunities for differentiation—where your business can offer something unique or superior.

Next, conduct a SWOT analysis of your competitors. This involves assessing their strengths, weaknesses, opportunities, and threats. Strengths might include a strong brand reputation or advanced technology, while weaknesses could be limited distribution channels or poor customer service. Opportunities might arise from emerging market trends or technological advancements, while threats could include new entrants or changing regulations. By understanding these elements, you can anticipate their moves and develop strategies to counteract their strengths or exploit their weaknesses.

With a clear picture of the competitive landscape, turn your focus inward to evaluate your own business. Consider your core competencies, resources, and capabilities. What do you do better than anyone else? What unique value do you offer to your customers? This self-assessment will help you identify your competitive advantage—the attribute or combination of attributes that allows you to outperform competitors.

Armed with insights from your competitive analysis and self-evaluation, it's time to define your market positioning. Positioning is about creating a distinct image of your brand in the minds of your target customers. It's the perception that sets you apart and influences purchasing decisions. Your positioning should be aligned with your unique value proposition and reflect your core brand values.

Craft a positioning statement that succinctly articulates your brand's unique value and market position. This statement should address your target audience, the category in which you compete, the benefit you provide, and what sets you apart from competitors. Here's a simple formula: "For [target audience], [brand] is the [category] that [unique benefit] because [reason to believe]." This positioning statement serves as a guiding light for all your marketing and branding efforts.

Once you've established your positioning, ensure it permeates every aspect of your business. From your product design and customer service to your marketing campaigns and corporate culture, your positioning should be consistently reflected in everything you do. This consistency not only strengthens your brand identity but also builds trust and loyalty among your customers.

Testing and refining your positioning is also essential. As markets evolve and customer preferences change, your positioning may need adjustment to stay relevant and competitive. Regularly seek feedback from customers, employees, and industry experts to gauge the effectiveness of your positioning and make necessary tweaks. This iterative process ensures that your brand remains aligned with market needs and expectations.

Embrace the power of storytelling to enhance your positioning. Stories are compelling tools for creating emotional connections and conveying complex ideas in an accessible way. Share your brand story, highlighting your mission, values, and the journey that led to your current position. Authentic stories resonate with customers, making your brand more relatable and memorable.

Finally, integrate your competitive analysis and positioning into your broader business strategy. Use them to inform product development, marketing initiatives, and customer engagement efforts. A well-defined competitive strategy helps you allocate resources effectively, prioritize initiatives, and make informed decisions that drive growth and profitability.

In the end, competitive analysis and positioning are not one-time tasks but ongoing processes that require vigilance and adaptability. By continuously monitoring the competitive landscape and refining your positioning, you ensure that your business remains agile and poised for success in an ever-changing market. These efforts lay the foundation for a robust and resilient brand that stands the test of time.

Leveraging Data for Strategic Decisions

In the ever-evolving landscape of modern business, data has emerged as a key driver of strategic decision-making. It offers insights that can transform how organizations operate, innovate, and compete. For beginners, understanding how to effectively leverage data can be the difference between thriving in a competitive market and merely surviving. This chapter will delve into practical ways to harness data for informed strategic decisions, providing a roadmap for using data to fuel growth and innovation.

The journey begins with recognizing the types of data available to your business. Broadly, data can be categorized into structured and unstructured forms. Structured data is highly organized and easily searchable, such as spreadsheets and databases containing numerical or categorical information. Unstructured data, on the other hand, includes more complex information like social media posts, customer reviews, or multimedia content. Both forms hold valuable insights, and understanding their potential is the first step toward leveraging them effectively.

Once you've identified the types of data at your disposal, it's crucial to establish a data collection strategy. Determine what information is most relevant to your business goals and how it will be gathered. For instance, if customer satisfaction is a priority, consider collecting feedback through surveys or monitoring social media channels. If you're focused on sales performance, track transaction data and customer interactions. The key is to align data collection efforts with your strategic objectives, ensuring that the information you gather is actionable and relevant.

With data in hand, the next step is analysis. Data analytics involves examining datasets to uncover patterns, trends, and correlations that can inform decision-making.

Depending on the complexity of your data and the questions you seek to answer, various analytical techniques can be employed. Descriptive analytics provides a summary of historical data, helping you understand past performance. Predictive analytics uses statistical models and machine learning algorithms to forecast future outcomes, enabling proactive decision-making. Prescriptive analytics goes a step further by suggesting actions based on predicted outcomes.

Visualization tools play a crucial role in making data insights accessible and understandable. By translating complex data sets into visual formats like charts, graphs, and dashboards, you can quickly identify trends and anomalies. These visualizations facilitate communication across your organization, allowing stakeholders to grasp key insights without needing deep technical expertise. Tools such as Tableau, Power BI, and Google Data Studio offer user-friendly platforms for creating dynamic visualizations that drive informed discussions.

One of the most powerful applications of data is in understanding customer behavior. By analyzing data from various touchpoints, such as website interactions, purchase history, and social media engagement, you can gain a comprehensive view of your customers' preferences and needs. This information can inform product development, marketing strategies, and personalized experiences, ultimately enhancing customer satisfaction and loyalty. For example, e-commerce platforms often use data analytics to recommend products based on past purchases, increasing the likelihood of repeat business.

Data also plays a critical role in optimizing operational efficiency. By monitoring key performance indicators (KPIs), businesses can identify areas for improvement and implement changes that enhance productivity and reduce costs. For instance, a manufacturing company might use data analytics to track production line performance, identifying bottlenecks and inefficiencies that can be addressed to streamline operations. Similarly, a service-based business might analyze employee performance data to optimize staffing levels and improve service delivery.

It's important to recognize that leveraging data for strategic decisions is an ongoing process. As your business evolves and external conditions change, so too will your data needs and priorities. Regularly revisiting your data strategy ensures that it remains aligned with your goals and adapts to new challenges and opportunities. This iterative approach allows you to continuously refine your strategies and maintain a competitive edge in the market.

While data presents immense opportunities, it also comes with responsibilities, particularly regarding privacy and security. As you collect and analyze data, prioritize compliance with relevant regulations, such as the General Data Protection Regulation (GDPR) or the California Consumer Privacy Act (CCPA). Implement robust data security measures to protect sensitive information and build trust with your customers. Transparency in data practices and a commitment to ethical use of data are essential components of a successful data strategy.

To maximize the potential of data-driven decision-making, foster a data-centric culture within your organization. Encourage employees at all levels to embrace data as a valuable asset and provide training to enhance data literacy. By equipping your team with the skills and confidence to interpret and utilize data, you empower them to contribute to strategic initiatives and drive innovation. A culture that values data fosters collaboration and creativity, enabling your organization to harness the full power of data insights.

Incorporating data into strategic decision-making is not without challenges. Common obstacles include data quality issues, integration complexities, and resistance to change. Addressing these challenges requires a proactive approach, including investing in data management systems, fostering collaboration between departments, and championing change management initiatives. By overcoming these hurdles, you pave the way for a seamless integration of data into your business processes, unlocking new avenues for growth and success.

In conclusion, leveraging data for strategic decisions is a transformative practice that can propel your business forward. By understanding the types of data available, developing a robust data strategy, and fostering a data-centric culture, you position your organization to make informed, impactful decisions. Embrace the potential of data, and you will find yourself better equipped to navigate the complexities of the modern business landscape, seize opportunities, and drive sustainable growth.

Chapter 3: Building an Effective Online Presence

Choosing the Right E-Commerce Platform

Embarking on the journey of setting up an online store begins with one of the most critical decisions—choosing the right e-commerce platform. This choice can significantly impact your business's functionality, scalability, and overall success. With a myriad of options available, each offering a unique set of features and benefits, finding the right fit requires a thoughtful approach. Here, we'll explore key considerations and steps to guide you in selecting the best platform for your needs.

Understanding your business requirements is the first step. Every e-commerce platform offers different features, and it's essential to identify which ones align with your business model and goals. Start by outlining your current needs and anticipating future demands. Consider factors such as the size of your product catalog, the complexity of your supply chain, and the level of customization you require. Are you looking for a platform that supports digital products, physical goods, or both? Do you need integration with existing systems like inventory management or accounting software? By clarifying your requirements, you create a roadmap that will help you evaluate potential platforms.

Next, consider the ease of use and user experience. For beginners, a platform with an intuitive interface and straightforward setup is crucial. You want a system that empowers you to manage your store without needing extensive technical expertise. Look for platforms that offer drag-and-drop functionality, customizable templates, and a user-friendly dashboard. The goal is to enable you to focus on running your business rather than getting bogged down by technical challenges.

Scalability is another vital consideration. As your business grows, your e-commerce platform should be able to accommodate increased traffic, expanded product offerings, and more complex operations. Evaluate how well each platform supports scalability, including the availability of advanced features and the ability to handle high volumes of transactions. Consider whether the platform offers seamless upgrades and the potential costs associated with scaling up. Choosing a platform with robust scalability ensures that your business can grow without unnecessary disruptions or limitations.

Don't overlook the importance of customization and flexibility. Every business is unique, and your e-commerce platform should allow you to tailor your store to reflect your brand identity and meet specific customer needs. Assess the level of customization each platform provides, from design elements to functionality. Can you modify the layout, add custom features, or integrate third-party apps? A platform that offers flexibility allows you to create a distinctive shopping experience that resonates with your audience and sets you apart from competitors.

Security is paramount in e-commerce, as customers entrust you with sensitive information such as payment details and personal data. Ensure that the platform you choose complies with industry security standards and offers robust protection against threats like data breaches and fraud. Look for features such as SSL certification, secure payment gateways, and regular security updates. A secure platform not only protects your business but also builds trust with your customers, fostering loyalty and repeat business.

The cost structure of an e-commerce platform can vary widely, and it's essential to understand the total cost of ownership before making a decision. Consider not only the upfront costs but also ongoing expenses such as transaction fees, hosting charges, and additional costs for premium features or plugins. Some platforms operate on a subscription model, while others charge based on sales volume or transaction count. Carefully evaluate how these costs align with your budget and financial projections to avoid unexpected expenses that could strain your resources.

Customer support and resources are also important factors to consider. As you navigate the complexities of setting up and managing an online store, having access to reliable support can make a significant difference. Evaluate the level of support each platform offers, including availability, response times, and the expertise of support staff. Additionally, consider the availability of resources such as tutorials, forums, and community groups. A platform with strong support and resources empowers you to troubleshoot issues and continuously improve your e-commerce operations.

Integration capabilities are another crucial aspect to evaluate. Your e-commerce platform should seamlessly integrate with other tools and systems you use, such as payment processors, social media, email marketing, and analytics platforms. This connectivity streamlines your operations and enhances your ability to gather valuable insights about your business and customers. Consider the ease of integration and whether the platform offers APIs or app marketplaces to extend functionality.

Mobile responsiveness is no longer optional in today's digital landscape. With a significant portion of consumers shopping on mobile devices, your e-commerce platform must provide a seamless mobile experience. Assess how well each platform supports mobile responsiveness, including the availability of mobile-friendly templates and the performance of the mobile shopping experience. A platform that prioritizes mobile usability ensures that you capture the growing segment of mobile shoppers and maximize sales opportunities.

Finally, take advantage of trial periods or demos offered by e-commerce platforms. This hands-on experience allows you to explore the features, interface, and performance of each platform in a real-world setting. Use this opportunity to test how well the platform meets your business requirements and how comfortable you feel using it. Pay attention to the platform's speed, reliability, and overall user experience, as these factors can significantly impact customer satisfaction and conversion rates.

Choosing the right e-commerce platform is a strategic decision that requires careful consideration of your business needs, goals, and resources. By evaluating factors such as ease of use, scalability, customization, security, cost, and support, you can make an informed choice that sets your business up for success. Remember that the best platform for your business is one that aligns with your vision, supports your growth, and enhances your ability to deliver exceptional value to your customers. With the right foundation in place, you'll be well-equipped to build a thriving online store that stands out in a competitive market.

Designing a User-Friendly Website

Creating a user-friendly website is a pivotal step for any business aiming to establish a compelling online presence. A well-designed website not only attracts visitors but also encourages them to engage, explore, and ultimately convert into loyal customers. The art of web design lies in balancing aesthetics with functionality, ensuring that users can effortlessly navigate and interact with your site. This chapter will guide you through the essential elements and strategies for constructing a website that captivates and serves its audience effectively.

Begin by understanding your audience. The foundation of a user-friendly website is rooted in knowing who your visitors are and what they seek. Conduct research to identify your target demographics, preferences, and behaviors. Are your users tech-savvy millennials or seasoned professionals? Do they prefer visual content over text, or are they seeking detailed information? This understanding will inform every aspect of your design, from layout and content to navigation and functionality.

Once you know your audience, focus on creating an intuitive navigation structure. A clear and logical navigation system guides users through your site, helping them find the information they need with minimal effort. Use descriptive labels for menu items and organize them in a hierarchical order that reflects the user's journey. Avoid cluttering the navigation bar with too many options; instead, prioritize the most important sections and use dropdown menus to categorize related content. Consistency is key—ensure that navigation elements are uniform across all pages to prevent confusion.

The layout of your website should be clean and organized, with a clear visual hierarchy that directs the user's attention to key elements. Utilize whitespace strategically to create a sense of balance and uncluttered space, allowing content to breathe and be easily digestible. Break up text with headings, bullet points, and images to enhance readability. The goal is to create a seamless flow that naturally guides users from one section to the next, making it effortless for them to absorb information.

Responsive design is essential in today's digital age, where users access websites from a variety of devices and screen sizes. A responsive website automatically adjusts its layout and functionality to provide an optimal viewing experience, whether on a desktop, tablet, or smartphone. Test your site across multiple devices and browsers to ensure compatibility and usability. Consider touch-friendly elements, such as larger buttons and swipe gestures, for mobile users. A responsive design not only improves user experience but also positively impacts search engine rankings, as search engines prioritize mobile-friendly sites.

The speed at which your website loads is another critical factor that influences user experience. Slow-loading pages frustrate users and increase bounce rates, leading to potential loss of business. Optimize your site for speed by compressing images, leveraging browser caching, and minimizing the use of plugins and scripts. Tools like Google PageSpeed Insights can help identify performance issues and provide recommendations for improvement. Fast-loading pages keep users engaged and encourage them to explore further.

Visual design plays a significant role in shaping the user's perception of your brand. Choose a color scheme that reflects your brand identity and evokes the desired emotions. Use typography that is legible and complements the overall design aesthetic. Consistent branding elements, such as logos and color palettes, create a cohesive look that reinforces brand recognition. Remember, the design should enhance the content, not overshadow it. Strive for a harmonious blend of visuals and text that captivates without overwhelming.

Content is the heart of your website, and it should be crafted with the user in mind. Provide valuable, relevant, and engaging content that addresses the needs and interests of your audience. Use clear and concise language, avoiding jargon or technical terms that may alienate users. Incorporate multimedia elements, such as videos and infographics, to enrich the content and cater to different learning styles. Regularly update your content to keep it fresh and relevant, encouraging repeat visits and fostering trust with your audience.

Implementing effective calls to action (CTAs) is crucial for guiding users toward desired actions, whether it's signing up for a newsletter, making a purchase, or contacting your team. CTAs should be prominently placed, easy to identify, and clearly communicate the next steps. Use action-oriented language that conveys urgency or value, such as "Get Started Today" or "Download Now." Test different variations of CTAs to determine what resonates best with your audience and drives conversions.

Accessibility is a vital consideration in web design, ensuring that all users, including those with disabilities, can access and interact with your site. Implement accessibility features such as alt text for images, keyboard navigation, and screen reader compatibility. Follow guidelines set by the Web Content Accessibility Guidelines (WCAG) to create an inclusive environment for all users. Prioritizing accessibility not only broadens your audience but also demonstrates a commitment to social responsibility and inclusivity.

Finally, leverage analytics to monitor user behavior and gather insights into how visitors interact with your site. Tools like Google Analytics provide valuable data on user demographics, traffic sources, and popular pages. Use this information to identify areas for improvement and make data-driven decisions to enhance the user experience. Regularly review your analytics to stay informed about changing user preferences and adjust your design strategy accordingly.

Designing a user-friendly website is an ongoing process that requires attention to detail and a willingness to adapt to evolving user needs. By focusing on intuitive navigation, responsive design, fast loading speeds, and engaging content, you create a seamless experience that delights users and encourages them to return. Embrace the principles of accessibility, simplicity, and consistency to build a website that not only meets but exceeds user expectations. With a user-centric approach, you lay the foundation for a successful online presence that drives engagement and fosters lasting connections with your audience.

Optimizing for Mobile Commerce

Mobile commerce, or m-commerce, has rapidly become an essential component of the retail landscape, offering consumers the convenience of shopping from the palm of their hands. As more people turn to their smartphones and tablets for purchasing goods and services, businesses must adapt by optimizing their online presence for mobile devices. This chapter will provide you with practical strategies to ensure your mobile commerce platform is not only functional but also engaging and efficient.

Understanding the behavior of mobile users is paramount. Mobile shoppers often exhibit different habits compared to desktop users; they tend to seek quick, seamless experiences and are frequently on the move. This means that your mobile site must be intuitive and easy to navigate, with minimal barriers between the user and their desired action. Start by examining your current mobile traffic and user behavior through analytics tools. Identify common paths users take and any potential drop-off points. This data will guide you in refining the mobile experience to better meet user expectations.

The first impression is crucial, and speed is a significant factor in shaping that impression. Mobile users are often impatient, and a slow-loading site can result in lost sales and frustrated customers. Optimize your mobile site for speed by compressing images, minimizing the use of large files, and reducing server response times. Implement accelerated mobile pages (AMP) to enhance load times, especially for content-heavy pages. Conduct regular performance tests to ensure your site remains fast and responsive, keeping users engaged and reducing bounce rates.

Responsive design is fundamental in creating a seamless experience across various devices. A responsive website automatically adjusts its layout and content to fit the screen size of the device being used. This ensures that whether a customer is using a smartphone, tablet, or desktop, they receive a consistent and user-friendly experience. Implement media queries in your CSS to define how content should be displayed on different devices, and prioritize the mobile experience when designing your site. This mobile-first approach ensures that essential elements are optimized for smaller screens, providing a more cohesive experience.

Simplifying navigation on your mobile site is another critical consideration. Mobile screens have limited space, so it's important to prioritize the most important elements and streamline the user journey. Use a hamburger menu or collapsible navigation to save space while still providing access to essential pages. Ensure that buttons and links are easily tappable, with enough space between them to prevent accidental clicks. Implement a sticky navigation bar that remains visible as users scroll, allowing them to quickly access key sections or actions.

Mobile commerce often involves on-the-go transactions, so optimizing the checkout process is essential for capturing sales. Simplify the checkout process by minimizing the number of steps required to complete a purchase. Offer guest checkout options to reduce friction and encourage conversions. Integrate mobile payment solutions such as Apple Pay, Google Pay, or PayPal, which allow users to complete transactions with a single tap. Ensure that form fields are easy to fill out on a mobile device, with features like autofill and real-time validation to streamline the process.

Personalization is a powerful tool in enhancing the mobile commerce experience. Leverage data and analytics to offer personalized recommendations, promotions, and content based on user behavior and preferences. Implement push notifications to engage users with timely and relevant messages, such as abandoned cart reminders or exclusive offers. Personalization not only increases user engagement but also drives conversions by delivering content that resonates with individual users.

Security is a top priority in mobile commerce, as users need to trust that their personal and payment information is safe. Ensure that your site is secure by using HTTPS, implementing strong data encryption, and adhering to industry security standards. Communicate your commitment to security by displaying trust badges and providing clear information about your privacy policies. A secure mobile commerce platform builds trust with users, encouraging them to complete transactions and return for future purchases.

Testing and optimization are ongoing processes in mobile commerce. Regularly conduct usability tests to identify areas for improvement and gather feedback from real users. Use A/B testing to evaluate changes and determine which variations lead to better performance and user satisfaction. Monitor key performance indicators (KPIs) such as conversion rates, bounce rates, and average order value to assess the effectiveness of your mobile strategy. Continuously iterating on your mobile site ensures that it remains relevant and competitive in a rapidly evolving marketplace.

Customer support is an integral part of the mobile commerce experience. Provide users with easy access to support options, such as live chat, email, or phone support. Implement self-service options like FAQs or chatbots to address common inquiries and reduce the burden on your support team. Ensure that support channels are mobile-friendly and responsive, allowing users to quickly get the help they need without interrupting their shopping experience.

Finally, consider the role of mobile apps in your overall mobile commerce strategy. While a responsive website is essential, a dedicated mobile app can offer additional features and benefits, such as offline access, enhanced personalization, and loyalty programs. Evaluate whether a mobile app aligns with your business goals and provides value to your customers. If so, invest in developing an app that complements your mobile site and enhances the overall user experience.

Optimizing for mobile commerce is not just about adapting to current trends; it's about anticipating the needs of your users and delivering exceptional experiences that meet those needs. By prioritizing speed, responsiveness, simplicity, and personalization, you create a mobile commerce platform that not only attracts but also retains customers. Embrace the mobile-first mindset, and you'll position your business for success in an increasingly mobile-driven world.

Creating Compelling Product Listings

A compelling product listing is the bridge between a potential customer and a purchase decision. It is the digital equivalent of a salesperson, tasked with capturing attention, conveying key information, and persuading the visitor to click "buy." Crafting such listings requires a blend of creativity, strategy, and empathy, ensuring that each product's unique features and benefits are presented in the most enticing way possible. This chapter will explore essential techniques to create product listings that resonate with customers and drive sales.

Begin by understanding the role of product listings within the broader context of your online store. This is not merely about showcasing a product; it's about storytelling. Each listing should tell a story about how the product can solve a problem, enhance a lifestyle, or fulfill a need. To achieve this, start by identifying your target audience. Who are they? What are their pain points and desires? This understanding will guide the tone and content of your listings, ensuring they speak directly to the intended audience.

A captivating product title is your first opportunity to make an impression. It should be clear, concise, and descriptive, providing essential details such as the brand, model, and key features. Avoid cluttering the title with excessive information, but ensure it includes keywords that potential customers are likely to search for. An effective title not only helps with search engine optimization (SEO) but also immediately communicates what the product is and why it matters.

The product description is where you have the opportunity to delve deeper into the story. This is your chance to highlight the unique selling points and benefits, painting a vivid picture of how the product fits into the customer's life. Use engaging language and varied sentence structures to maintain interest. Start with the most compelling features and benefits, then delve into technical details and specifications for those who seek them. Consider using bullet points for clarity and readability, especially when listing features or specifications.

Imagery plays a significant role in creating an engaging product listing. High-quality images provide a visual representation of the product, helping customers envision it in their lives. Include multiple images from different angles, showcasing key features and details. Consider lifestyle images that depict the product in use, as these can evoke emotions and aspirations. Ensure images are well-lit, clear, and professional, as poor-quality visuals can detract from the perceived value of the product.

Videos can further enhance product listings by providing dynamic, interactive content. A short video demonstration can showcase the product's functionality, highlight its benefits, and provide a real-world context. Videos are particularly effective for complex or innovative products that require explanation or demonstration. Keep videos concise and focused, ensuring they add value to the listing and are easily accessible on both desktop and mobile devices.

Incorporating customer reviews and testimonials can significantly bolster the credibility of your product listings. Social proof, in the form of user-generated content, provides authentic insights into the product's performance and quality. Encourage satisfied customers to leave reviews and consider featuring standout testimonials prominently in the listing. Address common concerns or questions raised in reviews by updating the product description or providing additional resources, such as FAQs or user guides.

Pricing is a critical component of product listings, and it should be presented transparently and competitively.

Clearly display the price, including any discounts or promotions, and consider offering multiple pricing tiers if applicable. If your product is part of a bundle or collection, highlight the value proposition of purchasing additional items together. Providing clear information about shipping costs, taxes, and return policies can further enhance trust and transparency.

SEO is a vital aspect of crafting effective product listings. By incorporating relevant keywords into titles, descriptions, and metadata, you improve the visibility of your products in search engine results. Conduct keyword research to identify terms that potential customers are using to find products like yours. Balance SEO with readability and engagement, ensuring that the listing remains natural and compelling for human readers.

Cross-selling and upselling opportunities can be woven into product listings to boost sales and average order value. Recommend complementary products or accessories that enhance the primary product's functionality or appeal. Use phrases like "Customers also bought" or "Complete the look" to suggest additional purchases. Ensure that these recommendations are relevant and genuinely add value to the customer's experience.

Finally, consider the mobile experience when designing product listings. With a significant portion of consumers shopping on mobile devices, it's crucial to ensure that listings are mobile-friendly. Optimize images and videos for smaller screens, and ensure that text is legible without excessive zooming or scrolling. A seamless mobile experience not only improves user satisfaction but also contributes to higher conversion rates.

Creating compelling product listings is a dynamic process that requires ongoing attention and refinement. Regularly review and update listings to reflect changes in inventory, pricing, or customer feedback. Stay informed about industry trends and emerging technologies that can enhance the presentation of your products. By prioritizing the needs and preferences of your customers, you create listings that not only attract but also convert, driving the success of your online store.

Enhancing User Experience and Navigation

Designing an intuitive and enjoyable user experience is critical to the success of any online platform. It is about creating a seamless journey that guides visitors effortlessly from entry to conversion. When users interact with your website, their experience should be as smooth as a well-paved road, free of potholes and detours. This is achieved not only through appealing visuals but also through strategic, user-centered navigation design.

Understanding the user journey begins with putting yourself in the shoes of your visitors. Consider their motivations, needs, and potential obstacles they might encounter. Start by mapping out the typical paths users take when interacting with your site. Are they searching for specific information, exploring product categories, or seeking customer support? Identify these journeys and ensure that your website is structured to facilitate them efficiently.

Navigation is the backbone of user experience. It should be intuitive, predictable, and consistent across all pages. The primary navigation bar should feature the most important sections of your site, allowing users to quickly access key areas. Use descriptive labels that clearly communicate the content of each section, avoiding jargon or ambiguous terms. Consider implementing breadcrumb trails to help users retrace their steps, providing a sense of orientation and control as they navigate deeper into the site.

A well-thought-out information architecture is crucial for effective navigation. Categorize content logically, grouping related items together in a way that makes sense to the user. Conduct user testing to validate your assumptions and refine the structure based on feedback. This process ensures that your site mirrors the mental models of your users, making it easier for them to find what they're looking for.

Search functionality is a valuable tool for enhancing user navigation, especially on content-rich sites. A well-designed search feature allows users to bypass navigation menus and go directly to the content they seek. Ensure that the search bar is prominently placed and easily accessible from any page. Implement features like autocomplete, synonym recognition, and filters to refine search results and improve accuracy. Analyzing search data can also provide insights into user behavior and highlight areas for content improvement.

Mobile responsiveness is an integral part of enhancing user experience, as a growing number of users access websites via mobile devices. Ensure that your site is fully responsive, adapting seamlessly to different screen sizes and orientations. Simplify navigation for mobile users by using a collapsible menu or hamburger icon. Prioritize touch-friendly elements with sufficient spacing to prevent accidental clicks. Mobile optimization not only improves user satisfaction but also boosts your site's search engine rankings.

Visual design elements play a significant role in user experience. Consistent branding, color schemes, and typography create a cohesive and professional appearance that enhances credibility. Use visual cues like icons and buttons to guide users and highlight interactive elements. A clean, uncluttered design with ample whitespace allows content to stand out and improves readability. Ensure that interactive elements provide feedback, such as hover effects or animations, to confirm user actions.

Speed is an essential component of user experience. Users expect fast-loading pages, and any delay can lead to frustration and abandonment. Optimize images and videos for web use, and minimize the use of heavy scripts or plugins that could slow down your site. Leverage browser caching, content delivery networks (CDNs), and efficient coding practices to improve load times. Regularly test your site's performance using tools like Google PageSpeed Insights to identify and address bottlenecks.

Personalization can greatly enhance user experience by delivering content and recommendations tailored to individual preferences. Leverage data analytics to understand user behavior and preferences, and use this information to customize their experience. Personalized product recommendations, content suggestions, and targeted promotions create a more engaging and relevant experience for users, encouraging repeat visits and conversions.

Accessibility is another critical aspect of user experience. Your site should be accessible to all users, including those with disabilities. Follow the Web Content Accessibility Guidelines (WCAG) to ensure that your site is usable by people with visual, auditory, or motor impairments. Implement features such as alt text for images, keyboard navigation, and screen reader compatibility. Prioritizing accessibility not only broadens your audience but also demonstrates a commitment to inclusivity.

Gathering user feedback is invaluable for continuous improvement of user experience. Implement tools such as surveys, feedback forms, or user testing sessions to collect insights directly from your audience. Analyze this feedback to identify pain points, areas for enhancement, and opportunities for innovation. Regularly updating and iterating on your design based on user feedback ensures that your site remains relevant and user-friendly.

Incorporating social proof elements, such as customer reviews, ratings, and testimonials, can also enhance user experience by building trust and credibility. Display genuine feedback prominently on product pages or in strategic locations throughout the site. Encourage satisfied customers to share their experiences, and respond to reviews to demonstrate engagement and transparency.

Finally, ensure that your site has a clear and compelling call to action (CTA) on each page. Whether it's signing up for a newsletter, making a purchase, or contacting your team, the CTA should be prominently placed and easy to understand. Use action-oriented language that conveys value and urgency, prompting users to take the next step in their journey.

Enhancing user experience and navigation is an ongoing process that requires attention to detail and a deep understanding of your users. By focusing on intuitive navigation, mobile optimization, visual design, speed, personalization, accessibility, and feedback, you create a website that not only meets but exceeds user expectations. A user-centric approach not only drives conversions and loyalty but also sets your business apart in a competitive digital landscape.

Chapter 4: Harnessing Digital Marketing and Advertising

Understanding Digital Marketing Channels

Navigating the landscape of digital marketing requires a keen understanding of the various channels at your disposal. Each channel offers unique opportunities to connect with your audience, promote your brand, and drive conversions. Mastering these channels means crafting a strategy that leverages their strengths and aligns with your business goals. This chapter will provide a comprehensive overview of key digital marketing channels, offering insights into their distinct features and best practices for effective use.

Search engine optimization (SEO) is a cornerstone of digital marketing, aimed at improving your website's visibility in search engine results pages (SERPs). SEO involves optimizing your website's content, structure, and technical aspects to align with the algorithms used by search engines like Google. This includes keyword research to identify terms your audience uses to find products or services like yours, as well as on-page optimization such as meta tags, headings, and alt text for images. Off-page SEO, including backlinks from reputable sites, also plays a crucial role in boosting your site's authority and ranking.

Pay-per-click (PPC) advertising offers a way to drive immediate traffic to your website through paid search engine placements. With PPC, you bid on keywords relevant to your business, and your ads appear when users search for those terms. PPC platforms like Google Ads allow for precise targeting based on demographics, location, and device. Crafting compelling ad copy and selecting the right keywords is essential for maximizing your return on investment (ROI). PPC campaigns offer measurable results, allowing you to track metrics such as click-through rates (CTR) and conversion rates to refine your strategy.

Social media marketing harnesses the power of platforms like Facebook, Instagram, Twitter, and LinkedIn to engage with your audience and build brand awareness. Each platform has its own unique user base and content style, so it's important to tailor your approach accordingly. Facebook, with its broad demographic reach, is ideal for community building and customer engagement, while Instagram's visual focus suits brands with strong imagery. LinkedIn offers opportunities for B2B marketing, connecting with industry professionals and thought leaders. Consistent posting, interaction with followers, and leveraging features like stories and live videos can enhance your social media presence.

Content marketing focuses on creating and distributing valuable, relevant content to attract and engage a target audience. This can take the form of blog posts, videos, infographics, podcasts, and more. The goal is to provide content that addresses the needs and interests of your audience, establishing your brand as a trusted resource. A well-executed content marketing strategy can improve SEO, drive traffic, and nurture leads through the sales funnel. Key to success is understanding your audience's preferences and delivering content that resonates with them, all while maintaining a consistent brand voice.

Email marketing remains one of the most effective channels for reaching your audience directly. It allows for personalized communication and nurturing relationships with subscribers. Building a strong email list is crucial, and this can be achieved through lead magnets, such as free downloads or exclusive offers. Crafting compelling subject lines and content that provides value to your readers is essential for high open and click-through rates. Email automation tools can help streamline campaigns, segment your audience, and deliver targeted messages based on user behavior and preferences.

Affiliate marketing involves partnering with individuals or companies (affiliates) who promote your products in exchange for a commission on sales. This channel can expand your reach and tap into new audiences, leveraging the influence and credibility of affiliates. Successful affiliate marketing requires clear communication, fair commission structures, and providing affiliates with the tools and resources they need to succeed. Tracking performance and ensuring compliance with legal and ethical standards is also important for maintaining a successful affiliate program.

Influencer marketing leverages individuals with a strong social media presence and influence in your industry to promote your brand. Influencers can provide authentic endorsements and reach niche audiences that might be difficult to access through traditional marketing channels. Selecting the right influencers is key; they should align with your brand values and have an engaged following that matches your target demographic. Building genuine relationships with influencers and collaborating on creative content can enhance brand visibility and drive conversions.

Each digital marketing channel offers its own set of advantages and challenges. A successful strategy often involves a mix of channels, tailored to your business goals and audience preferences. It's important to continually monitor and analyze the performance of each channel, using analytics tools to track key metrics and adjust your approach as needed. This data-driven approach allows you to optimize your marketing efforts, ensuring that resources are allocated effectively and goals are met.

The interconnected nature of digital marketing channels means that a change in one area can impact others. For example, a successful content marketing campaign can boost SEO by driving traffic and earning backlinks, while social media promotion can amplify the reach of your content. Understanding these interdependencies allows for more holistic and integrated marketing strategies, maximizing the potential of each channel.

By mastering digital marketing channels, you position your business to thrive in the digital landscape. Embrace the opportunities each channel presents, and stay informed about emerging trends and technologies. With a strategic and flexible approach, you can effectively engage your audience, foster connections, and drive sustainable growth.

Search Engine Optimization (SEO) Strategies

Search engine optimization (SEO) is a critical component of any online strategy, transforming the visibility and reach of your website in the vast digital landscape. By leveraging SEO, businesses can enhance their site's ranking in search engine results pages (SERPs), driving organic traffic and increasing the likelihood of conversions. This chapter delves into effective SEO strategies that can elevate your online presence, tailored specifically for beginners eager to make their mark.

Understanding the fundamentals of SEO begins with recognizing the role search engines play in connecting users with relevant content. Search engines use algorithms to evaluate and rank websites based on various factors, with the ultimate goal of delivering the most pertinent results to users. By aligning your website with these algorithms, you can improve your ranking and visibility. Keyword research is the cornerstone of this process, as it identifies the terms and phrases your target audience uses when searching for products or services like yours. Tools such as Google Keyword Planner or SEMrush can help you discover high-volume, low-competition keywords that are relevant to your niche.

Once you have identified key terms, integrating them naturally into your website content is crucial. This involves optimizing page titles, meta descriptions, and headers to include targeted keywords, ensuring that they accurately reflect the content on each page. However, it's important to avoid keyword stuffing, which can lead to penalties from search engines. Instead, focus on creating informative and engaging content that provides value to your audience while naturally incorporating keywords.

On-page SEO extends beyond keywords to encompass the overall structure and user experience of your website. A well-organized site with logical navigation not only aids user experience but also helps search engines crawl and index your content more effectively. Use a clear hierarchy with main categories and subcategories, and implement internal linking to connect related pages. This structure not only enhances usability but also distributes authority throughout your site, improving the ranking potential of individual pages.

Technical SEO is another vital aspect, addressing the backend elements of your site that impact search engine visibility. Site speed is a critical factor, as slow-loading pages can deter users and lead to higher bounce rates. Optimize images, leverage browser caching, and use content delivery networks (CDNs) to enhance load times. Additionally, ensure your site is mobile-friendly, as search engines prioritize mobile-optimized sites in their rankings. Implementing a responsive design ensures your site adapitates seamlessly to different screen sizes, providing a consistent experience across devices.

Securing your website with HTTPS encryption is also essential, as it protects user data and contributes to search engine ranking signals. Search engines prioritize secure sites, and displaying the HTTPS protocol can build trust with users. Regularly audit your site for broken links, duplicate content, and crawl errors using tools like Google Search Console, addressing any issues promptly to maintain a healthy site.

Content is king in the realm of SEO, and regularly updating your site with fresh, relevant content can significantly impact your ranking. Publishing high-quality blog posts, articles, and guides that address the interests and needs of your audience not only attracts visitors but also encourages them to spend more time on your site. This increased engagement can signal to search engines that your site is valuable and authoritative, boosting its ranking potential. Consider incorporating multimedia elements like images, videos, and infographics to enrich your content and enhance user experience.

Off-page SEO strategies focus on building your site's reputation and authority through external signals. Backlinks from reputable sites serve as endorsements of your content, indicating to search engines that your site is trustworthy and valuable. Building a strong backlink profile requires a proactive approach, seeking opportunities for guest blogging, collaborations, and partnerships within your industry. Engaging with your audience on social media platforms can also amplify your content's reach and attract natural backlinks.

Local SEO is particularly important for businesses with a physical presence, as it targets users searching for products or services within a specific geographic area. Optimizing your Google My Business profile, ensuring consistent name, address, and phone number (NAP) information across online directories, and encouraging customer reviews can enhance your local search visibility. Local SEO not only increases foot traffic to your physical location but also builds brand awareness within your community.

Analyzing and measuring the impact of your SEO efforts is crucial for ongoing success. Tools like Google Analytics provide insights into your site's performance, tracking metrics such as organic traffic, bounce rates, and conversion rates. Regularly reviewing these metrics allows you to identify trends, assess the effectiveness of your strategies, and make data-driven adjustments to your approach. SEO is an evolving field, with search engine algorithms continually updating to improve the quality of search results. Staying informed about industry trends, algorithm updates, and best practices ensures your strategies remain relevant and effective.

SEO is a long-term investment that requires patience and persistence. Results may not be immediate, but consistent effort can yield significant returns in terms of increased visibility, traffic, and conversions. By implementing a comprehensive SEO strategy that combines on-page, off-page, and technical elements, you position your website for sustained success in the competitive digital landscape. Embrace the journey, adapt to changes, and continue refining your approach, and you will unlock the full potential of search engine optimization.

Social Media Marketing for E-Commerce

Social media has revolutionized the way businesses connect with their audience, offering e-commerce platforms the ability to engage directly with potential customers in real-time. This dynamic and interactive environment presents unique opportunities for e-commerce brands to build relationships, drive traffic, and ultimately boost sales. Understanding the nuances of social media marketing is essential for any business looking to thrive in the digital age.

Choosing the right platforms is the first step in crafting an effective social media strategy. Not all platforms are created equal, and each has its own demographic and style of engagement. Facebook, with its vast user base and diverse demographic, serves as a versatile platform for community building and customer interaction. Instagram, on the other hand, is highly visual and appeals to a younger audience, making it ideal for brands with strong imagery and aesthetics. Twitter offers real-time engagement and is perfect for brands that thrive on timely interactions and updates. Meanwhile, Pinterest functions as a visual discovery engine, perfect for showcasing products and driving traffic to e-commerce sites. LinkedIn, though primarily a professional network, can be leveraged for B2B e-commerce and thought leadership.

Once you've identified the platforms that align with your target audience, the next step is developing content that resonates. Content is the lifeblood of social media marketing, and creating a variety of content types keeps your audience engaged. High-quality images, videos, and graphics are essential, as they capture attention quickly in a fast-scrolling environment. Storytelling through images and captions can humanize your brand, making it relatable and memorable. User-generated content, such as customer reviews and photos, can also build trust and authenticity, showcasing real-life use of your products.

Consistency is key to maintaining an active presence on social media. Develop a content calendar to plan and schedule posts in advance, ensuring a steady stream of content. This not only keeps your audience engaged but also frees up time to interact with them. The timing of your posts can significantly impact their reach and engagement; therefore, analyze your audience's behavior to determine the best times to post. Tools like Hootsuite or Buffer can assist in scheduling and managing posts across multiple platforms.

Engagement is at the heart of social media marketing. It's not just about broadcasting messages but fostering two-way communication with your audience. Promptly responding to comments, messages, and mentions shows that you value your customers' input and are attentive to their needs. Encourage interaction by asking questions, running polls, or hosting live sessions. Contests and giveaways can also boost engagement, encouraging followers to share your content and expand your reach.

Advertising on social media platforms offers targeted opportunities to reach new audiences and drive conversions. Facebook and Instagram Ads, for instance, allow you to target users based on demographics, interests, and behaviors, ensuring your ads reach the most relevant audience. Crafting compelling ad copy and visuals is crucial for capturing attention and encouraging clicks. Utilize retargeting strategies to reach users who have previously interacted with your brand, reminding them of products they've viewed or abandoned in their cart.

Analytics play a crucial role in refining your social media strategy. Regularly reviewing metrics such as engagement rates, reach, and conversion rates provides insights into what's working and what needs improvement. Each platform offers its own analytics tools, providing data on post performance, audience demographics, and user behavior. Use this data to adjust your content strategy, focusing on types of content and posting times that yield the best results. A data-driven approach allows for continuous improvement and optimization of your social media efforts.

Influencer marketing is another powerful strategy within social media marketing. By partnering with influencers who have a strong presence and credibility in your niche, you can tap into their audience and gain exposure. Choose influencers whose values align with your brand and whose followers match your target demographic. Authenticity is key; collaborations should be genuine and reflect a true endorsement of your products. Influencer campaigns can take various forms, from sponsored posts to product reviews or takeovers, each offering a unique way to showcase your brand.

Social media platforms are constantly evolving, introducing new features and trends that can enhance your marketing efforts. Staying informed about these changes allows you to adapt and incorporate new strategies into your approach. Features like Instagram Stories, Reels, and Shopping, or Facebook Live, offer innovative ways to engage with your audience and promote your products. Experimenting with these features can set your brand apart and keep your content fresh and exciting.

Creating a seamless integration between your social media presence and your e-commerce site is essential for driving conversions. Ensure that your social media profiles link directly to your website, making it easy for users to explore and purchase your products. Social media platforms like Instagram and Facebook offer shopping features that allow users to browse and buy products without leaving the app, streamlining the purchasing process and reducing friction.

Incorporating customer feedback and insights gained from social media interactions can inform your overall business strategy. Listening to your audience provides valuable information about their preferences, pain points, and expectations. Use this feedback to refine your product offerings, improve customer service, and enhance the overall customer experience. By aligning your business strategies with the needs and desires of your audience, you create a more personalized and satisfying experience for your customers.

Social media marketing for e-commerce is a dynamic and multifaceted endeavor that requires creativity, strategy, and adaptability. By choosing the right platforms, crafting engaging content, fostering genuine interactions, and leveraging advertising and analytics, you can create a powerful social media presence that drives brand awareness and sales. As the digital landscape continues to evolve, staying flexible and open to new opportunities will ensure your social media marketing remains effective and impactful.

Pay-Per-Click (PPC) Advertising

Pay-per-click (PPC) advertising stands as a pivotal element in the digital marketing arsenal, providing businesses with the ability to reach potential customers quickly and effectively. This form of online advertising allows advertisers to place ads on search engine results pages, social media platforms, and other websites, paying a fee each time their ad is clicked. For beginners, understanding the intricacies of PPC can seem daunting, but with a strategic approach, it becomes a powerful tool for driving traffic and conversions.

To embark on a successful PPC campaign, one must first grasp the foundational concepts. At its core, PPC is a model of internet marketing where advertisers bid on keywords relevant to their target audience. These keywords trigger their ads to appear when users search for related terms. The bidding process involves advertisers determining how much they are willing to pay for each click, with search engines like Google using a combination of bid amount and ad quality to determine ad placement. This system ensures that users are presented with the most relevant ads, enhancing their experience and increasing the likelihood of engagement.

Crafting compelling ad copy is a critical component of PPC success. An effective ad captures attention, communicates value, and encourages action, all within a limited character count. Begin by identifying the unique selling proposition (USP) of your product or service—what sets it apart from the competition? Incorporate this USP into your ad copy, using strong, action-oriented language to prompt clicks. Including a clear call-to-action (CTA) is essential, guiding users toward the desired action, whether it's making a purchase, signing up for a newsletter, or downloading a resource.

Keyword research is the backbone of any PPC campaign. Identifying the right keywords ensures that your ads reach the most relevant audience, those actively searching for what you offer. Utilize tools like Google Keyword Planner or Ubersuggest to discover keywords with high search volume and low competition. Long-tail keywords, which are longer and more specific phrases, often yield better results as they attract more qualified leads. Continuously monitor and refine your keyword list, adding new terms and removing underperforming ones to optimize your campaign's effectiveness.

Landing page optimization plays a crucial role in converting clicks into customers. When users click on your ad, they should be directed to a landing page that aligns with the ad's message and offers a seamless path to conversion. The landing page should be visually appealing, easy to navigate, and contain relevant content that fulfills the promise made in the ad. A clear and concise headline, engaging visuals, and a compelling CTA are key elements that contribute to an effective landing page. Additionally, ensure that your landing page loads quickly and is mobile-friendly, as slow-loading or unresponsive pages can lead to high bounce rates and lost opportunities.

Targeting and segmentation are vital aspects of PPC advertising, allowing you to reach specific groups within your broader audience. Platforms like Google Ads and Facebook Ads offer advanced targeting options, enabling you to tailor your campaigns based on demographics, location, interests, and even behaviors. By segmenting your audience, you can create personalized ad experiences that resonate more deeply with users, increasing the likelihood of conversion. Regularly analyze your audience segments and adjust targeting parameters to ensure your ads remain relevant and effective.

Budget management is another critical consideration in PPC advertising. Determining how much to allocate to your PPC campaigns involves balancing your marketing goals with your financial resources. Start by setting a daily or monthly budget based on your overall marketing strategy and adjust it as needed based on campaign performance. It's important to monitor your spending closely and ensure that your budget is being used efficiently. Tools like Google Ads' Budget Planner can help you estimate costs and allocate resources effectively, maximizing your return on investment (ROI).

Analytics and tracking are indispensable tools for measuring the success of your PPC campaigns. By tracking key performance indicators (KPIs) such as click-through rates (CTR), conversion rates, and cost per acquisition (CPA), you gain valuable insights into what's working and what needs improvement. Google Analytics and platform-specific reporting tools provide detailed data on user interactions, helping you identify trends and make data-driven decisions. Regularly reviewing and analyzing this data allows you to optimize your campaigns, refine your strategies, and achieve better results over time.

A/B testing, also known as split testing, is a powerful technique for optimizing PPC campaigns. By creating multiple versions of an ad or landing page and testing them against each other, you can determine which elements resonate most with your audience. Test variables such as headlines, ad copy, images, and CTAs to identify the most effective combinations. Implementing the winning variations can lead to improved performance and higher conversion rates. Continuously testing and iterating on your campaigns ensures that they remain fresh and effective, adapting to changes in user behavior and market trends.

Understanding the competitive landscape is essential for PPC success. Analyzing competitors' ad strategies provides valuable insights into industry trends and consumer preferences. Tools like SEMrush and SpyFu allow you to research competitors' keywords, ad copy, and spending patterns, helping you identify opportunities and gaps in your own strategy. By staying informed about the competition, you can make informed decisions and adjust your approach to maintain a competitive edge.

PPC advertising is not a one-size-fits-all solution, and what works for one business may not work for another. It's important to approach PPC with a mindset of experimentation and adaptability. Be willing to try new strategies, learn from failures, and celebrate successes. With dedication and a commitment to continuous improvement, PPC can become a highly effective component of your digital marketing strategy, driving traffic, increasing conversions, and contributing to your overall business growth.

Content Marketing and Brand Storytelling

Crafting a compelling narrative through content marketing is an art that can transform a brand from a mere name into a memorable story. Brand storytelling is about more than just selling a product or service; it's about creating an emotional connection with your audience, one that resonates deeply and fosters loyalty. In the digital age, where consumers are inundated with information, a well-told story can set a brand apart, making it not only visible but unforgettable.

Every brand has a story waiting to be told. It begins with understanding the essence of what your brand stands for, its values, mission, and the journey that brought it to life. This narrative becomes the foundation upon which all content is built, guiding the tone, style, and message that you communicate to the world. A strong brand story is authentic, aligning with the core principles of your business and reflecting the interests and values of your audience. This authenticity builds trust, an invaluable asset in cultivating long-term relationships with customers.

To begin crafting your brand story, consider the human element behind your brand. Who are the people driving it forward? What challenges have they faced, and what triumphs have they achieved? Personal stories add depth and relatability to your brand, transforming abstract concepts into tangible experiences. Showcase the passion and dedication of your team, highlighting the individuals who contribute to your brand's success. These stories humanize your brand, making it relatable and approachable to your audience.

Once the core narrative is established, the next step is to weave this story into your content marketing strategy. Content marketing is the vehicle through which your brand story is delivered, encompassing a variety of formats such as blog posts, videos, podcasts, and social media updates. Each piece of content should serve a purpose, whether it's educating, entertaining, or inspiring your audience. By consistently delivering content that aligns with your brand story, you reinforce your message and strengthen your brand identity.

Visual storytelling plays a crucial role in content marketing, capturing attention and conveying emotions in ways that words alone cannot. High-quality images, videos, and infographics can bring your brand story to life, creating an immersive experience for your audience. Consider creating behind-the-scenes videos that offer a glimpse into your brand's operations, or infographics that illustrate key milestones in your brand's history. These visual elements not only enhance engagement but also make your story more shareable, expanding your reach across digital platforms.

Engagement is at the heart of effective content marketing, and storytelling provides the perfect opportunity to invite your audience into the conversation. Encourage user-generated content by inviting customers to share their own stories and experiences with your brand. This not only builds community but also provides valuable insights into how your brand is perceived. User-generated content adds authenticity and diversity to your brand story, showcasing real-life interactions and testimonials that resonate with potential customers.

Social media platforms are powerful tools for amplifying your brand story, offering direct channels to engage with your audience. Tailor your content to suit the unique characteristics of each platform, whether it's the visual focus of Instagram, the real-time engagement of Twitter, or the professional network of LinkedIn. Use these platforms to share not only your own content but also stories from your community, creating a dialogue that strengthens your brand's presence and influence.

Measuring the success of your content marketing efforts is essential to refining your strategy and ensuring it resonates with your audience. Analytics tools provide valuable data on engagement metrics such as likes, shares, comments, and clicks, offering insights into which content formats and topics are most effective. Regularly review this data to assess the impact of your brand storytelling, making adjustments as needed to optimize performance and reach your marketing goals.

As the digital landscape evolves, so too should your brand story. Stay attuned to changes in consumer behavior, industry trends, and technological advancements, adapting your narrative to remain relevant and engaging. This flexibility ensures that your brand continues to connect with your audience, maintaining its position as a trusted and beloved entity in their lives.

Brand storytelling through content marketing is a journey, one that requires creativity, authenticity, and a deep understanding of your audience. By embracing the power of narrative, you can transform your brand into a story that captivates, inspires, and endures. This connection not only drives immediate engagement but also fosters a lasting relationship with your audience, turning customers into advocates and ensuring the continued success of your brand.

Chapter 5: Leveraging Technology for Operational Efficiency

Implementing Inventory Management Systems

Efficient inventory management is the backbone of any successful e-commerce operation. It ensures that businesses can meet customer demand without overstocking or understocking, both of which can have significant financial implications. Implementing an inventory management system is a transformative step that can streamline operations, reduce costs, and enhance customer satisfaction.

The first consideration in implementing an inventory management system is selecting the right software that aligns with your business needs. There are numerous options available, each offering a range of features tailored to different types of businesses. It's essential to evaluate your specific requirements, such as the size of your inventory, the scale of your operations, and the complexity of your supply chain. Look for a system that offers real-time tracking, automated reordering, and integration with your existing e-commerce platform to ensure a seamless transition.

Real-time inventory tracking is a critical feature of modern inventory management systems. This functionality allows businesses to monitor stock levels in real time, providing visibility into the location and status of each item. By having up-to-date information, businesses can make informed decisions, respond quickly to changes in demand, and reduce the risk of stockouts or excess inventory. Implementing barcode scanning or RFID technology can further enhance accuracy and efficiency, minimizing human error and streamlining the tracking process.

Automated reordering is another significant advantage of an inventory management system. By setting predefined thresholds for each product, the system can automatically generate purchase orders when stock levels fall below the specified point. This automation reduces the administrative burden on staff, ensures that inventory levels are maintained, and prevents disruptions in the supply chain. Moreover, automated reordering can be tailored to account for seasonal fluctuations or promotional campaigns, enabling businesses to adapt to changing market conditions.

Integration with suppliers is a vital component of effective inventory management. Establishing strong relationships with suppliers and integrating their systems with your inventory management software can lead to more efficient and reliable operations. This integration facilitates seamless communication, allowing for real-time updates on product availability, lead times, and order status. By collaborating closely with suppliers, businesses can negotiate better terms, reduce lead times, and improve overall supply chain performance, ultimately enhancing customer satisfaction.

Inventory forecasting is a valuable tool that helps businesses anticipate future demand based on historical data and market trends. By analyzing past sales patterns, seasonality, and external factors, businesses can predict upcoming demand and adjust inventory levels accordingly. Accurate forecasting minimizes the risk of overstocking or understocking, optimizing cash flow and reducing holding costs. Implementing an inventory management system with robust forecasting capabilities allows businesses to plan effectively and respond proactively to changes in the market.

Data analytics play a crucial role in inventory management, providing insights into various aspects of the supply chain. Using data analytics, businesses can identify trends, measure performance, and uncover areas for improvement. For example, analyzing sales data can reveal which products are top performers and which may require reevaluation. Similarly, tracking inventory turnover rates can highlight opportunities for optimizing stock levels. By leveraging data analytics, businesses can make informed decisions that drive efficiency and profitability.

Ensuring accuracy in inventory records is paramount to effective inventory management. Discrepancies between recorded and actual stock levels can lead to costly errors and inefficiencies. Regular audits and cycle counts are essential practices for maintaining accuracy and accountability. Cycle counting involves counting a small subset of inventory on a regular basis, ensuring that records remain accurate without the need for a full physical inventory count. Implementing systematic processes for audits and cycle counts helps identify discrepancies early and allows for timely corrective action.

Training staff on inventory management practices and the use of the new system is a key step in successful implementation. Employees need to understand the importance of accurate record-keeping, proper handling of inventory, and effective use of the inventory management software. Comprehensive training ensures that staff are equipped with the skills and knowledge necessary to operate the system efficiently, reducing the likelihood of errors and maximizing the benefits of the system.

Scalability is an important consideration when selecting an inventory management system. As businesses grow, their inventory management needs may change, requiring a system that can adapt to increased complexity and volume. Choosing a system with scalable features ensures that it can accommodate future growth, supporting the business as it expands into new markets or introduces new product lines. A scalable system provides flexibility and longevity, making it a wise investment for long-term success.

Technology and innovation continue to shape the landscape of inventory management, offering new opportunities to enhance efficiency and accuracy. Emerging technologies such as artificial intelligence and machine learning are increasingly being integrated into inventory management systems, providing advanced analytics and predictive capabilities. These technologies enable businesses to automate routine tasks, optimize inventory levels, and improve decision-making processes. Staying informed about technological advancements ensures that businesses can leverage the latest tools and techniques to maintain a competitive edge.

Implementing an inventory management system is a strategic move that can transform your e-commerce operations. By selecting the right software, automating processes, integrating with suppliers, and leveraging data analytics, businesses can achieve greater efficiency, reduce costs, and enhance customer satisfaction. With a focus on accuracy, scalability, and continuous improvement, an effective inventory management system becomes a cornerstone of success in the fast-paced world of e-commerce.

Streamlining Order Fulfillment Processes

Order fulfillment is the heartbeat of any e-commerce operation, a complex orchestra of processes that ensures customers receive their products efficiently and accurately. In the competitive landscape of online shopping, where customer expectations are high and patience is short, streamlining these processes can make a significant difference. By refining order fulfillment, businesses not only enhance customer satisfaction but also improve operational efficiency and reduce costs.

The journey of order fulfillment begins the moment a customer places an order on your website. This initiates a series of actions, each crucial to ensuring a seamless delivery experience. The first step in this journey is order processing, which involves verifying payment, checking inventory availability, and confirming the order details. Automation can play a vital role here, reducing manual errors and speeding up the process. Implementing an order management system (OMS) that integrates with your e-commerce platform can automate these tasks, ensuring orders are processed swiftly and accurately.

Once an order is processed, the next step is picking and packing—a stage where efficiency and accuracy are paramount. A well-organized warehouse layout can significantly impact the speed and ease with which items are picked. Grouping frequently purchased items together, organizing products logically, and ensuring that inventory is clearly labeled can streamline the picking process. Utilizing technology such as barcode scanners or pick-to-light systems can further enhance accuracy and speed, reducing the likelihood of errors and ensuring that customers receive the correct items.

Packing is more than just placing items in a box; it's an opportunity to reinforce your brand and enhance the customer experience. Thoughtful packaging not only protects products during transit but also creates a memorable unboxing experience for the customer. Consider using branded materials, personalized notes, or eco-friendly packaging options to make a positive impression. Additionally, ensuring that packages are correctly labeled with the right shipping information is crucial to avoid delays and misdeliveries.

Shipping is a critical component of order fulfillment, and selecting the right carriers and shipping methods can have a significant impact on delivery times and costs. Offering a variety of shipping options, such as standard, expedited, and international, allows customers to choose the service that best meets their needs. Negotiating favorable rates with carriers and leveraging volume discounts can reduce shipping costs and improve margins. Moreover, providing customers with tracking information enhances transparency and allows them to monitor the progress of their delivery, reducing anxiety and increasing satisfaction.

Returns are an inevitable aspect of e-commerce, and having a streamlined returns process is essential for maintaining customer trust and loyalty. A clear and simple returns policy, prominently displayed on your website, sets expectations and reduces confusion. Automating the returns process, from generating return labels to tracking returned items, can improve efficiency and reduce the burden on customer service teams. By analyzing return data, businesses can identify common reasons for returns and take proactive measures to address underlying issues, reducing the overall return rate.

Communication is a cornerstone of effective order fulfillment. Keeping customers informed at every stage of the fulfillment process helps manage expectations and build trust. Automated email notifications, triggered at key stages such as order confirmation, shipment, and delivery, provide reassurance and transparency. A customer portal on your website, where customers can track their orders and manage returns, offers an additional layer of convenience and control.

Technology is a powerful enabler of streamlined order fulfillment processes. From warehouse management systems (WMS) that optimize inventory placement and picking routes, to customer relationship management (CRM) systems that track customer interactions and preferences, technology provides the tools needed to enhance efficiency and accuracy. Regularly reviewing and updating your technology stack ensures that you leverage the latest innovations and maintain a competitive edge.

Scalability is an important consideration when designing order fulfillment processes. As your business grows, your fulfillment operations must be able to handle increased order volumes without sacrificing speed or accuracy. This may involve expanding warehouse capacity, hiring additional staff, or investing in automated solutions such as robotics or conveyor systems. Planning for scalability ensures that your fulfillment processes can support your business's growth trajectory, providing a consistent and reliable customer experience.

Continuous improvement is a core principle of successful order fulfillment. Regularly reviewing your processes, soliciting feedback from customers and employees, and analyzing key performance metrics can uncover opportunities for optimization. Metrics such as order processing time, picking accuracy, and on-time delivery rates provide valuable insights into the efficiency and effectiveness of your fulfillment operations. Embracing a culture of continuous improvement encourages innovation and fosters a commitment to excellence.

Order fulfillment is a multifaceted process that requires careful coordination and attention to detail. By streamlining these processes, businesses can enhance customer satisfaction, improve operational efficiency, and drive growth. With a focus on automation, technology, and continuous improvement, e-commerce businesses can build a fulfillment operation that not only meets but exceeds customer expectations.

Utilizing Customer Relationship Management (CRM) Tools

In the world of e-commerce, where competition is fierce and customer expectations are continually evolving, utilizing Customer Relationship Management (CRM) tools is essential for building and maintaining strong relationships with your clientele. CRM tools are more than just a repository for customer information; they are a strategic asset that can drive customer satisfaction, loyalty, and business growth. By harnessing the power of these tools, businesses can gain valuable insights, streamline operations, and deliver personalized experiences that resonate with customers.

At the heart of CRM lies the ability to centralize customer data, providing a comprehensive view of each customer's interactions with your brand. This includes purchase history, communication records, preferences, and feedback. By consolidating this information, businesses can better understand their customers' needs and tailor their offerings accordingly. Imagine a customer who frequently buys outdoor gear from your online store. With a CRM system, you can track their preferences for specific brands or types of equipment, allowing you to offer personalized recommendations and promotions that align with their interests.

Personalization is a key advantage of using CRM tools, enabling businesses to create unique and engaging experiences for each customer. By leveraging data on customer behavior and preferences, businesses can craft targeted marketing campaigns that speak directly to individual needs and desires. Personalized email campaigns, for example, can significantly increase engagement and conversion rates by delivering relevant content that resonates with recipients. A CRM system can automate the process of segmenting your audience and sending tailored messages, ensuring that your marketing efforts are both efficient and effective.

CRM tools also play a crucial role in enhancing customer service, a vital component of building long-term relationships. With access to a customer's complete interaction history, customer service representatives can provide informed and empathetic support, addressing issues quickly and effectively. This comprehensive view allows representatives to anticipate potential problems and offer proactive solutions, demonstrating a commitment to customer satisfaction. Additionally, CRM systems often include features such as ticketing and case management, streamlining the process of tracking and resolving customer inquiries.

Sales teams can greatly benefit from CRM tools, which provide valuable insights into the sales pipeline and customer behavior. By tracking leads, opportunities, and sales activities, CRM systems offer a clear view of the sales process, helping teams prioritize efforts and close deals more efficiently. Sales representatives can use CRM data to identify upselling or cross-selling opportunities, tailoring their approach to meet the specific needs of each customer. This data-driven approach not only enhances sales performance but also builds stronger relationships by delivering value at every stage of the customer journey.

The integration of CRM tools with other business systems, such as e-commerce platforms, marketing automation tools, and analytics software, creates a seamless flow of information across the organization. This integration ensures that all teams have access to accurate and up-to-date customer data, enabling consistent and coordinated interactions. For example, integrating a CRM system with an e-commerce platform allows businesses to track a customer's online behavior, such as browsing history and abandoned carts, providing opportunities to re-engage and convert potential customers.

Data security and privacy are critical considerations when implementing CRM tools. Customers trust businesses with their personal information, and it is the responsibility of the business to protect that data. Ensure that your CRM system complies with relevant data protection regulations, such as the General Data Protection Regulation (GDPR) in the European Union or the California Consumer Privacy Act (CCPA) in the United States. Implementing robust security measures, such as encryption and access controls, safeguards customer data and builds trust with your audience.

Choosing the right CRM tool for your business involves evaluating your specific needs and objectives. There are numerous CRM solutions available, each offering a range of features and capabilities. Consider factors such as ease of use, scalability, customization options, and integration capabilities when selecting a CRM system. It's important to choose a tool that aligns with your business goals and can adapt to changing requirements as your business grows.

Training and onboarding are essential steps in ensuring the successful adoption and utilization of CRM tools within your organization. Employees need to understand how to use the system effectively, from entering and managing customer data to generating reports and insights. Providing comprehensive training and ongoing support helps employees feel confident and empowered in using the CRM system, maximizing its benefits for both the business and its customers.

Continuous improvement is a fundamental principle in leveraging CRM tools to their fullest potential. Regularly review and analyze CRM data to identify trends, measure performance, and uncover opportunities for optimization. Metrics such as customer acquisition cost, customer lifetime value, and retention rates provide valuable insights into the effectiveness of your CRM strategy. By embracing a culture of continuous improvement, businesses can refine their approach, enhance customer experiences, and drive sustainable growth.

In conclusion, utilizing CRM tools is a strategic advantage that can transform the way businesses interact with their customers. By centralizing data, personalizing experiences, and enhancing customer service, CRM systems enable businesses to build lasting relationships and achieve long-term success. With careful selection, integration, and continuous improvement, CRM tools become a powerful ally in navigating the complexities of the modern e-commerce landscape.

Automating Business Operations

In the dynamic world of business, the ability to respond swiftly and efficiently to market demands is crucial for success. Automation presents a powerful solution, enabling businesses to streamline operations, reduce manual workload, and enhance productivity. By strategically implementing automation, businesses can focus on innovation and growth while maintaining a competitive edge.

Automation begins with identifying repetitive and time-consuming tasks that can be optimized. These tasks often include data entry, order processing, inventory management, and customer support. By automating these processes, businesses can minimize human error, increase efficiency, and free up valuable time for employees to engage in more strategic activities. For example, automating data entry through integration with customer relationship management (CRM) systems ensures that customer information is accurately captured and updated in real time, eliminating the need for manual input and reducing the risk of errors.

Order processing is another area where automation can have a significant impact. Automating the workflow from order receipt to fulfillment can drastically reduce processing times and improve accuracy. With an automated system, orders are automatically verified, inventory levels are checked, and shipping labels are generated, resulting in faster fulfillment and enhanced customer satisfaction. This seamless process not only improves operational efficiency but also allows businesses to scale more effectively as order volumes increase.

Inventory management is a critical component of business operations, and automation can provide valuable insights and control. Automated inventory systems track stock levels in real time, offering visibility into product availability and demand trends. This information enables businesses to optimize stock levels, reducing the risk of overstocking or stockouts. By automating reorder processes based on predefined thresholds, businesses ensure they maintain optimal inventory levels without manual intervention, ultimately reducing carrying costs and improving cash flow.

Customer support is an area where automation can enhance both efficiency and customer experience. Implementing chatbots and automated response systems allows businesses to handle routine inquiries and provide instant support to customers. These tools can be programmed to answer frequently asked questions, guide users through troubleshooting processes, and escalate complex issues to human representatives. By automating basic support tasks, businesses can ensure that customers receive timely assistance while allowing support teams to focus on resolving more complex issues.

Marketing automation is another powerful tool that can drive business growth. By automating marketing campaigns, businesses can deliver personalized content to their audience at scale. Automated email marketing systems can segment audiences based on behavior, preferences, and demographics, sending targeted messages that resonate with recipients. This personalization enhances engagement and conversion rates, allowing businesses to maximize the return on their marketing investment. Additionally, automation tools can track campaign performance, providing valuable data for refining strategies and optimizing results.

The integration of automation tools across various business systems is essential for creating a cohesive and efficient operation. By connecting systems such as CRM, enterprise resource planning (ERP), and marketing automation platforms, businesses can ensure a seamless flow of information across departments. This integration eliminates data silos, enhances collaboration, and enables informed decision-making based on comprehensive data insights. For example, integrating CRM and ERP systems allows sales teams to access real-time inventory data, providing accurate information to customers and reducing the risk of overpromising.

Security and compliance are important considerations when implementing automation. Ensuring that automated systems comply with relevant regulations, such as data protection and industry-specific standards, is crucial for maintaining trust and avoiding legal issues. Implementing robust security measures, such as encryption and access controls, protects sensitive data and ensures the integrity of automated processes. Regular audits and assessments help identify potential vulnerabilities and ensure that systems remain secure and compliant.

Selecting the right automation tools involves evaluating your business's specific needs and goals. There is a wide range of automation solutions available, each offering different features and capabilities. Consider factors such as ease of integration, scalability, and customization when choosing tools that align with your business objectives. It's important to select tools that can adapt to changing requirements and support future growth, ensuring a long-term return on investment.

Training and support are essential for successful automation implementation. Employees need to understand how to use and manage automated systems effectively. Providing comprehensive training and ongoing support ensures that staff are equipped with the skills and knowledge necessary to leverage automation tools to their fullest potential. This support fosters confidence and competence, allowing employees to embrace automation as an asset rather than a challenge.

Continuous improvement is a fundamental principle in leveraging automation for business success. Regularly reviewing and analyzing automated processes can uncover opportunities for optimization and innovation. Metrics such as processing time, error rates, and customer satisfaction provide insights into the effectiveness of automation efforts. By embracing a culture of continuous improvement, businesses can refine their approach, enhance efficiency, and drive sustainable growth.

Automation is a transformative force that can revolutionize business operations. By identifying opportunities for automation, integrating tools across systems, and focusing on continuous improvement, businesses can streamline processes, reduce costs, and enhance the customer experience. With thoughtful implementation and strategic use of automation, businesses can unlock new levels of efficiency and innovation, positioning themselves for long-term success in a competitive marketplace.

Integrating AI and Machine Learning

Integrating AI and machine learning into business operations heralds a new era of efficiency, insight, and innovation. As these technologies continue to evolve, they offer unprecedented opportunities for businesses to enhance processes, predict trends, and deliver personalized experiences. For those venturing into this realm, understanding the foundational elements and practical applications of AI and machine learning is key to unlocking their potential.

The journey begins with understanding the distinction between AI and machine learning. AI refers to the broader concept of machines performing tasks that would typically require human intelligence, such as understanding language, recognizing patterns, and solving problems. Machine learning, a subset of AI, focuses on the ability of systems to learn from data and improve over time without being explicitly programmed. By leveraging these technologies, businesses can automate complex tasks, uncover insights, and drive data-driven decision-making.

One of the most impactful applications of AI in business is in data analysis and decision support. With the vast amounts of data generated daily, businesses can struggle to extract actionable insights. AI systems excel at processing large datasets, identifying patterns, and generating insights that can inform strategic decisions. For example, AI can analyze customer behavior data to identify purchasing patterns, enabling businesses to optimize marketing strategies and inventory management.

Predictive analytics, powered by machine learning, takes data analysis a step further by forecasting future trends based on historical data. This capability is invaluable for businesses seeking to anticipate market shifts, customer preferences, and potential risks. Retailers, for instance, can use predictive analytics to forecast demand for specific products during peak seasons, ensuring they stock the right inventory levels. By anticipating trends, businesses can make proactive adjustments that enhance competitiveness and profitability.

Personalization is another area where AI and machine learning shine. By analyzing customer data, these technologies can deliver tailored experiences that resonate with individual preferences and behaviors. In e-commerce, personalized product recommendations can enhance the shopping experience, leading to increased customer satisfaction and higher conversion rates. Machine learning algorithms analyze browsing and purchase history to suggest products that align with a customer's interests, creating a more engaging and relevant interaction.

In customer service, AI-powered chatbots and virtual assistants offer efficient and cost-effective support solutions. These tools can handle routine inquiries, provide instant responses, and guide customers through common issues. By automating basic support tasks, businesses can ensure timely assistance and free up human agents to address more complex queries. Additionally, AI can enhance customer service by analyzing sentiment in customer interactions, allowing businesses to gauge satisfaction levels and make improvements.

The integration of AI and machine learning into supply chain management offers transformative benefits. These technologies can optimize logistics by predicting demand fluctuations, identifying bottlenecks, and recommending efficient routing strategies. For manufacturers, AI can enhance production processes by monitoring equipment performance and predicting maintenance needs, reducing downtime and improving efficiency. By optimizing supply chain operations, businesses can reduce costs, improve delivery times, and enhance overall service quality.

Implementing AI and machine learning requires careful planning and consideration of several factors. Data quality is paramount, as these technologies rely on accurate and comprehensive datasets to function effectively. Businesses must ensure they have robust data collection and management processes in place, maintaining data integrity and security. Additionally, selecting the right AI tools and platforms that align with your business objectives is crucial. Consider factors such as ease of integration, scalability, and customization when evaluating solutions.

Ethical considerations and compliance with regulations are essential when deploying AI and machine learning. Businesses must ensure that their use of these technologies aligns with relevant legal and ethical standards, such as data privacy and non-discrimination. Implementing transparency measures, such as explainable AI, helps build trust by providing insights into how AI systems make decisions. Regular audits and assessments can ensure compliance and address potential ethical concerns.

Training and upskilling employees is a critical component of successful AI integration. Employees need to understand how AI systems work, how to interpret their outputs, and how to leverage them in decision-making processes. Providing comprehensive training and fostering a culture of continuous learning empowers employees to embrace AI as a valuable tool rather than a threat. This support encourages innovation and ensures that businesses fully capitalize on the benefits of AI and machine learning.

Continuous improvement and iteration are fundamental principles in leveraging AI and machine learning. As these technologies evolve, businesses must remain agile and adaptable, regularly reviewing and refining their strategies. Monitoring key performance indicators and gathering feedback from stakeholders provides insights into the effectiveness of AI initiatives. By embracing a mindset of continuous improvement, businesses can refine their approach, enhance performance, and maintain a competitive edge.

Integrating AI and machine learning represents a significant opportunity for businesses to enhance operations, drive innovation, and deliver exceptional value to customers. By understanding the capabilities and considerations of these technologies, businesses can implement solutions that transform processes and unlock new potential. With thoughtful planning, ethical considerations, and a commitment to continuous improvement, AI and machine learning become powerful allies in navigating the complexities of the modern business landscape.